TABLE OF CONTENTS

This Page Intentionally Blank

INTRODUCTION

Coercion, the threatened or limited use of force to induce an adversary to change

its behavior, continues to be a significant element of United States (US) foreign policy.[1]

Successful coercion requires a consistent, credible and capable military instrument of

national power. US leaders enable credibility-the power of inspiring belief-and

capability-the ability or potential for indicated use-by developing a sound coercive

strategy prior to initiating threats or action. These leaders display consistency-adhering

to one method of conduct-by maintaining pressure until reaching an acceptable end state.

The US has relied on threats and use of military force to back diplomatic efforts on

numerous occasions since the Cold War ended, with mixed results. Many believed,

"liberated from the danger that military action will lead to confrontation with a rival

superpower, the United States is now more free to intervene."[2] However, rather than

being free to intervene, the US has discovered other nations continue to resist coercion.

Lacking a clear strategy and displaying hesitance or unwillingness to use the level of

force required to achieve objectives are primary reasons for coercion delay or failure in

US attempts. To improve the potential for successful coercion in future foreign policy, a

full understanding of the elements and effects of coercion along with why, when and how

to threaten or employ US military force are essential.

Studying coercion theory provides knowledge of its components, their effects and

capabilities. Armed with this knowledge, officials can learn from historical coercion

---

[1] Daniel Byman and Matthew Waxman, *The Dynamics of Coercion: American Foreign Policy and the Limits of Military Might* (New York, Cambridge University Press, 2002), 1.

[2] Richard N. Haass, *Intervention: The Use of American Military Force in the Post-Cold War World*, revised edition (Washington DC: Brookings Institution Press, 1999), 3.

cases and better employ a coercion strategy in the future. Coercion includes the components of deterrence and compellence. Deterrence can include a general threat to prevent actions of others or specific threats designed to discourage specific actions. Merriam-Webster defines deter as "to turn aside, discourage or prevent from acting." However, when another nation will not be deterred, the US may need to compel the behavioral change. The US Joint Chiefs of Staff describe compel as "to maintain a threat--or actual use--of lethal or nonlethal force to establish control and dominance, effect behavioral change, or enforce cessation of hostilities, peace agreements, or other arrangements."[3]

Once the US decides it has to use coercion to impose change, US leadership must develop a coercion strategy. First, the level of US national interests and the objective must be determined. The situation can range from a vital interest threatening the security of the nation, to an important national interest that affects the national well-being, to humanitarian and other interests, which drive US intervention due to values.[4] The level of interest and objective should determine the elements of national power used and what limits will be placed upon that power. Second, US leadership should plan the coercion strategy. The various capabilities from the diplomatic, informational, economic and military elements of power will be analyzed and selected. It is also during plan development that leaders must determine how high they intend to raise the stakes to achieve success, which may end with military force. Finally, US officials must state the demand clearly and consistently. Clarity ensures adversary understanding and expected

---

[3] US Joint Chiefs of Staff, *Joint Operation Planning,* Joint Publication 5-0 (Washington DC: Joint Chiefs of Staff, August 11, 2011), III-30.

[4] US President, *A National Security Strategy for a New Century* (Washington DC: Government Printing Office, October 1998), 5-6.

action, while consistency shows the will to act, giving credibility to the threatened force. Though US officials will place limits on its force, it is essential the adversary believe force will be applied to the level and conviction needed, while remaining unaware of any US self-imposed limitations.

As mentioned, the US has many instruments of national power including military, economic, diplomatic, and other information tools, each of which can be used to help coerce another nation.[5] However, the known or implied threat of US military power is always present. The term military power includes "the elements which contribute directly or indirectly to the capacity to coerce, kill, and destroy."[6] To achieve the best effects from this power, leaders must understand why, when and how they will employ the power. This determination is made in policy before the coercion occurs and must be clear and consistent. This clarity of purpose will make US official policy known domestically and internationally when or if military actions are required.

History provides cases where the US attempted to coerce other nations using military power. Interventions in Panama, Bosnia, Kosovo, and Libya are reviewed to look for common themes and examples in the post-Cold War era. Coercion failed in Panama and Libya, while it was partially successful in Bosnia and Kosovo. Problems range from being hesitant to get involved, reluctant to use force, stating early public limitations on force available, unclear objectives, inconsistent demands, no consequence for violations of mandates, and providing incentives when no reward was earned. These

---

[5] David E. Johnson, Karl P. Mueller, and William H. Taft, *Conventional Coercion Across the Spectrum of Operations: The Utility of USMilitary Forces in the Emerging Security Environment* (Santa Monica: Rand, 2002), 7.

[6] Henry E. Eccles, *Military Power in a Free Society,* (Newport: Naval War College Press, 1979), 53.

identified lessons can help military leaders better inform political leadership when the next coercive use of military force becomes necessary.

The following chapters begin by defining coercion and providing background to the evolving theory. How and why to develop a strategy to implement coercion and how to measure success or failure are discussed. Next, thoughts on the use of military power are provided, showing the doctrine, policies and perceptions that shape how this instrument of national power is used. Though often hesitant to commit to the use of force in coercion, history shows the US has done so in over 50 percent of the opportunities since the Cold War began, with neither the public nor Congress preventing its use.[7]

As mentioned, a study of four recent US coercion attempts provide examples of US involvement in terms of goals, stated strategy, means employed, and resulting end state. An analysis follows to measure success in the cases studied in regard to consistency of demand, credible expectation of the use of threatened US military force, and employment of a capable military force. Lessons from this analysis will aid in making future threats of military force more consistent and credible. Successfully coercing nations to comply with US demands requires a clear strategy, with realistic and consistent goals, backed by credible means to issue threats of escalating force that are capable of imposing the stated objectives. A consistent, credible, and capable military instrument of power is essential to future coercion success.

---

[7] James D. Meernik, *The Political Use of Military Force in US Foreign Policy* (Burlington: Ashgate Publishing Company, 2004), 15-16.

CHAPTER 1: THEORY AND ELEMENTS OF COERCION

Sun Tzu stated, "For to win one hundred victories in one hundred battles is not the acme of skill. To subdue the enemy without fighting is the acme of skill."[1] To this end, nations will try to change the thinking or behavior of an adversary to defend interests without need for war. Coercion, in the context of force backing diplomacy provides a way to accomplish adversary behavioral change with limited or no armed hostility.

To effectively coerce, leaders must understand the definition and elements of coercion in order to apply pressure on the adversary to achieve desired objectives. The definition and elements follow, leading into discussion of a coercion strategy to achieve desired objectives with consistent, credible and capable force. Armed with this knowledge, the value of coercion and the use of force in United States (US) foreign policy are explored.

What is Coercion?

Many scholars have defined coercion to show how diplomacy can influence another nation to act or change its behavior. During much of the Cold War between US-led Western nations and Soviet Union-led communist nations, diplomacy was dominated by the threat of nuclear weapons to deter actions. The small or limited interest wars of Korea and Vietnam called into question whether deterrence was a complete explanation to cover the realities of politics between nations.[2] In his book, *Arms and Influence*, Professor Thomas Schelling brought coercion into the discussion.

---

[1] Sun Tzu, *The Art of War*, trans. Samuel Griffith (New York: Oxford University Press, 1971), 77.

[2] Daniel Byman and Matthew Waxman, *The Dynamics of Coercion: American Foreign Policy and the Limits of Military Might* (New York, Cambridge University Press, 2002), xiii.

According to Schelling, coercion "is the threat of damage, or of more damage to come that can make someone yield or comply."[3] Schelling recognized "the power to hurt has been, throughout history, a fundamental character of military force and fundamental to the diplomacy based upon it."[4] Rational actors will naturally desire to avoid pain, leading them to find ways to prevent experiencing this pain. Daniel Byman and Matthew Waxman further define coercion as "the use of threatened force, and at times the limited use of actual force to back up the threat, to induce an adversary to behave differently than it otherwise would."[5] This definition furthered the idea of threatened or actual use of force while adding the idea of changing the adversary's behavior rather than focusing on compliance with a simple demand.

Robert Pape adds to behavior change reasoning by defining coercion as "efforts to change the behavior of a state by manipulating costs and benefits."[6] Pape's definition brings to light the rational decision making process the adversary must use to determine if the intended objectives are worth the potential cost for non-compliance. Additionally, Johnson, Mueller and Taft define coercion as "causing someone to choose one course of action over another by making the choice preferred by the coercer appear more attractive than the alternative, which the coercer wishes to avoid."[7] This definition clarifies the possibility that inducements can also coerce a nation rather than threats alone. The use of inducements in compliment with threats, commonly known as a "carrot and stick"

---

[3] Thomas Schelling, *Arms and Influence* (New Haven: Yale University Press, 1966), 3.

[4] Ibid., 33.

[5] Byman and Waxman, 30.

[6] Robert A. Pape, *Bombing to Win: Air Power and Coercion in War* (Ithaca: Cornell University Press, 1996), 4.

[7] David E. Johnson, Karl P. Mueller, and William H. Taft, *Conventional Coercion Across the Spectrum of Operations* (Santa Monica: Rand, 2002), 7.

approach to diplomacy, is often used to resolve disputes as it lends better to compromise.[8] However, these thoughts on coercion do not complete the discussion.

In their updated version of *The Limits of Coercive Diplomacy*, Alexander George and William Simons acknowledge that coercion in diplomacy, which they label coercive diplomacy, "is essentially a diplomatic strategy, one that relies on the threat of force rather than the use of force to achieve an objective."[9] This definition focuses more on threat rather than actual use of force to influence an adversary. George also separates coercive diplomacy into offensive and defensive methods in order to show that aggressively using threats of military power is not the best way to achieve objectives. According to George, "such offensive uses of coercive threats are better designated by the term blackmail strategy."[10] He chooses to deemphasize the offensive aspect of coercion to "emphasize the possibility of a more flexible diplomacy that can employ rational persuasion and accommodation as well as coercive threats to encourage the adversary either to comply with the demands or to work out an acceptable compromise."[11] The emphasis on a defensive nature of coercion, such as using incentives instead of threats, often fits better with American values of respecting the rights of others rather than creating the impression the US always forces solutions. Schelling points out a difficulty with our nation being unaggressive, whose announced

---

[8] Alexander L. George and William E. Simons, *The Limits of Coercive Diplomacy* (Boulder: Westview Press, 1994), 16.

[9] Ibid., 2.

[10] Ibid., 7.

[11] Ibid., 7.

aim is to contain rather than roll back, and has led to the lack of conventional terminology for more active kinds of threats.[12]

Although the cited definitions of coercion vary, the central theme is consistent. Coercion is a diplomatic strategy to induce or compel an adversary to behave in a certain way. As Carl von Clausewitz pointed out in his work, *On War*, "if the enemy is to be coerced, you must put him in a situation that is even more unpleasant than the sacrifice you are calling on him to make."[13] Clausewitz was speaking of actions during war, but his thought is equally relevant to coercion prior to war. In attempting to change or reverse the course of action of an adversary, the coercer must credibly show the adversary continuing unwanted action will not be allowed. A better understanding of coercion begins by covering its compellence and deterrence elements.

Compellence

Thomas Schelling coined the term compellence to better define the use of force in actively making an adversary comply with a demand. "Compellence is inducing his withdrawal, or his acquiescence, or his collaboration by an action that threatens to hurt, often one that could not forcibly accomplish its aim but that, nevertheless, can hurt enough to induce compliance."[14] This definition describes a method of taking action to achieve an objective without automatically resorting to war. Rather, the adversary gets to evaluate the conditions and choose to alter the unwanted behavior or face additional pain.

"Compellence attempts to make the target change its behavior in accordance with the coercer's demands—for example, to halt an invasion, to withdraw from disputed

---

[12] Schelling, 71.

[13] Carl von Clausewitz, *On War*, ed. and trans. Michael Howard and Peter Paret (Princeton: Princeton University Press, 1976), 85.

[14] Schelling, 79-80.

territory, or to surrender."[15] The coercer is taking an active or offensive role to force the adversary to respond, but not necessarily committing actual force. Typically, compellence is not an open-ended threat, but will include a deadline or ultimatum to bind the threat. Threats can be general or specific, such as "until you do X, I will do Y" or "unless you do X by my deadline, I will do Y."[16] To successfully compel an adversary with these threats requires a high level of effort and commitment by the nation to use military force. This commitment makes compellence more difficult for a nation to use, but allows the coercer the advantage of initiative in determining progress toward resolution. An additional reason compellence is more difficult than deterrence is "a state that is forced to change its behavior often faces the loss of prestige that comes from having publicly succumbed to pressure from another power."[17] The leadership of that government may not be able to accept this loss of reputation with its domestic power base or reputation with others, leading it to resist longer even in the face of certain defeat.

The two fundamental types of compellence used are denial and punishment.[18] The two terms are explained now as they are often used to compel an adversary, even though as types of coercion they can also apply to deterrence. As pointed out by Byman and Waxman, "in practice compellence is difficult to distinguish from deterrence," as any threat can be stated in compellent or deterrent means.[19] To best show how these theories blur in practice, Byman and Waxman provide an illustration shown on the following page:

---

[15] Johnson, Mueller, and Taft, 13.

[16] Ibid., 14.

[17] George and Simons, 84.

[18] Pape, 13-14.; Johnson, Mueller, and Taft, 16-17.

[19] Byman and Waxman, 7-8.

As mentioned previously, the context of the situation must be taken into account to determine which category best applies, realizing each may play a role.

Denial seeks to convince the adversary that resisting the coercer's demands will be unsuccessful.[21] This form of coercion attempts to convince the adversary it is pointless to resist as his power will be outmatched and ultimately result in loss of the objective. Even if the adversary chooses to continue pursuit of his objectives and is initially successful, the coercer's force will arrive to defeat the adversary and reverse the gains. Essentially, denial attempts to "render impotent an adversary's strategy for winning a crisis or conflict."[22] In that light, the coercer must understand the intentions of

_____

[20] Ibid., 8.

[21] Johnson, Mueller, and Taft, 16.

[22] Byman and Waxman, 78.

the adversary and identify the means at his disposal. Armed with that knowledge, the coercer can threaten the adversary by denying the strategy.

According to Pape, "denial operates using military means to prevent the target from attaining its political objectives or territorial goals."[23] This paper is concerned with the military as an instrument of coercion; however, it is possible to use other instruments of national power in denial, such as economic sanctions. The goal is to convince the adversary that pursuit, or continued pursuit of his goals is hopeless. Denial often focuses on threatening to defeat an adversary on the battlefield, but can include other means depending on the adversary's strategy.[24] Ultimately, success or failure of denial will depend on many factors and success will also depend upon coercer aims.

"Denial works when adversary leaders recognize that they cannot gain benefits and will continue to pay costs if they do not concede."[25] This realization may not be known or accepted by the adversary quickly; therefore, once a threat of denial is made, the coercer must remain committed. Adversary leadership must realize, and agree; their strategy has failed and believe the coercer can continue pressure as long as necessary to end the conflict.[26] Pressures from within the adversary government may require them to hold out as long as possible to maintain support; therefore, consistency, credibility, and committed capability from the coercer are essential.

---

[23] Pape, 13.

[24] Johnson, Mueller, and Taft, 16.

[25] Byman and Waxman, 78.

[26] Ibid., 82.

Punishment

Threats of punishment can also compel an adversary to meet coercer demands. The coercer tries to make the adversary believe the cost of pursuing an objective will be greater than the value of the perceived gains. "In its purest form, punitive coercion does not limit the enemy's ability to act but instead seeks to destroy the will to do so by making the effort appear too expensive to be worthwhile."[27] The coercer can threaten the adversary in many ways, such as bombing national infrastructure or striking other key nodes of importance. The threat of punishment is hoped to make the adversary fear the potential result of failing to meet coercer demands.

Coercion by threat of punishment does raise the costs or risks to civilian populations.[28] The costs can be raised by striking enemy population centers, as suggested by Giulio Douhet,[29] or it could mean targeting infrastructure, fielded forces or other national assets. Essentially, punitive threats are communicated to convey to the adversary what the coercer intends to do if the adversary fails to comply. Therefore, threats must be credible and believable in order to achieve coercive desires. Sun Tzu provides great insight in working to achieve coercive success: "what is of supreme importance in war is to attack the enemy's strategy, next best is disrupt his alliances, next best to attack his army. The worst policy is to attack cities, attack cities only when there is no other alternative."[30] Given this advice and the rules by which the US prosecutes

---

[27] Johnson, Mueller, and Taft, 16.

[28] Pape, 13.

[29] Giulio Douhet, *The Command of the Air,* trans. Dino Ferrari (North Stratford: Ayer Company Publishers, Inc., 2002), 20.

[30] Sun Tzu, 77-78.

war, it is safe to expect any threat will continue to follow this advice. However, rather than make coercive threats, sometimes it is better to deter adversary behavior or actions.

Deterrence

Deterrence is an element of coercion that takes place prior to action by an adversary. Like compellence, it also works to convince the adversary to change intentions; however, it is a more passive or defensive approach. According to Alexander George and Richard Smoke, "deterrence is simply the persuasion of one's opponent that the costs and/or risks of a given course of action he might take outweigh its benefits."[31] In deterrence, the choice for action is placed upon the adversary before action occurs. The deterrent threat is communicated to the adversary prior to action being taken, to encourage the adversary to maintain status quo. Robert Pape argues deterrence is apart from compellence for the reason the former seeks to prevent action where the latter seeks to alter action that has already occurred.[32] The lines between deterrence and compellence often blur as shown earlier in Figure 1. It therefore remains accurate to say that both elements of coercion work complementary, as the situation requires. Failure of deterrence will likely escalate to compellence, as countries increase pressure.

Deterrence occurs in the mind of the adversary where he must evaluate and perceive that the costs outweigh the gains if action is to be prevented. Deterrence can be accomplished using many means, military or non-military, but the means must be communicated such that the adversary is aware in order to use the threat in calculations.[33] As Schelling points out, "Deterrence is about intentions, not just estimating enemy

---

[31] Alexander L. George and Richard Smoke, *Deterrence in American Foreign Policy: Theory and Practice* (New York: Columbia University Press, 1974), 11.

[32] Pape, 4.

[33] Johnson, Mueller, and Taft, 12-13.

intentions but influencing them. The hardest part is communicating our own intentions."[34] Clear communication of intent, commitment, capability and means can be the factors determining success or failure. To further complicate deterrence, it can be applied in several contexts. Types of deterrence, including general, immediate and extended, apply to the context of the situation. While the act of deterrence is not changed in these cases, the conditions of employment are different.

General Deterrence

Byman and Waxman state, "general deterrence involves preventing an action, whether it was planned or not; general deterrent threats are always present to some degree."[35] A good example of general deterrence is the US possession of nuclear weapons. Many potential aggressors are likely dissuaded from attacking the US due to the available retaliatory capability these weapons provide coupled with not knowing exactly when and how the US would use these weapons. Though difficult to prove who is deterred by this threat, the possession of nuclear weapons provides a general deterrent capability, which is not necessarily directed at any specific nation or immediate danger.

Immediate Deterrence

Immediate deterrence is a threat directed at a specific or planned event.[36] In this context, an actor levies a specific threat, such as military force, against an adversary to prevent a specific act. The US and Soviet missile crisis of 1962 provides an example, when the Soviets began placing nuclear missiles on the island of Cuba. The US general deterrence against the Soviet Union shifted to immediate deterrence when President

---

[34] Schelling, 35.

[35] Byman and Waxman, 6-7.

[36] Ibid., 6-7.

Kennedy ordered Soviet missiles removed, announced a US quarantine of Cuba and stated if any Soviet missiles were launched against a Western Hemisphere target from Cuba, the full retaliation of the US would be directed against the Soviet Union.[37] This example shows the blurring lines of deterrence and compellence, where the quarantine compelled removal, immediate deterrence prevented use of the missiles from Cuba. The key point in immediate deterrence is the direct response to a specific event.

Extended Deterrence

Extended deterrence explains the situation larger nations often find themselves in when protecting smaller or weaker nations. Extended deterrence attempts to deter attacks against allies or outside interests rather than deterring attacks against the state itself.[38] Examples of this include allies within the North Atlantic Treaty Organization (NATO), where an attack on one is considered an attack on all. In extended deterrence, the adversary must believe the deterring state values the obligation enough to follow through with the threat. A lack of perceived commitment could lead the adversary to choose the aggressive act because the protector nation's stakes are thought not high enough to risk war, such as North Korea's decision to invade South Korea in 1950.[39] However, even if the coercive threat is believed, the adversary may resist or counter the threat.

Defying Coercion

As with war, coercion is not a one-sided contest and the adversary has the ability to provide inputs to any situation. Since coercion is the attempt to alter adversary decision making, it is normal to assume the adversary may choose a course of action

---

[37] Stephen J. Cimbala, *The Dead Volcano: The Background and Effects of Nuclear Complacency* (Westport, CT: Praeger Publishers, 2002), 223.

[38] Johnson, Mueller, and Taft, 12.

[39] George and Smoke, 146-148.

counter to the coercer's desired action. The adversary may decide to use threat or actual use of force to change the coercer's actions or test resolve. The target of coercion can seek his own allies to apply military, economic or territorial threats of their own against the coercer.[40] Alternatively, the adversary can work to minimize the effect the coercer's threats would have on the nation or impair coercer allied support. Ultimately, as in a chess game, each move will correspond with a countermove until the game is complete.

An example of defying coercion is provided with Israel, France and Britain's efforts against Egypt over the Suez Canal in 1956. Despite threats of attack, Egypt nationalized the canal, leading Israel, Britain and France to attack Egypt. In response, Egypt sank ships in the canal to effectively close the canal, exactly what the coercing nations were attempting to avoid.[41] To coerce an adversary, the coercer must prepare for counteractions and understand the level of commitment required. Along with understanding actions and commitment, the coercer must develop a successful strategy.

Coercion Strategy

Being the largest or even the strongest nation does not guarantee successful coercion. If that were true, weaker nations would always do as directed by the stronger. As previously identified, coercion attempts to convince the adversary nation to change objectives or behavior, therefore the decision calculus to acquiesce resides within the decision-making of the coerced nation. Thus, in determining a strategy to coerce an adversary, the rational decision making of the adversary must be understood. In order to help determine the best approach to coercion, many authors have used cost-benefit ideas

---

[40] Johnson, Mueller, and Taft, 22.

[41] Byman and Waxman, 42-43.

16

or models.[42] Essentially, there are key elements of coercive threats that can aid in focusing the efforts of the coercer. Four basic elements are benefits, costs, probabilities and perceptions.[43]

Benefits allude to the expected gain the adversary intends to receive from the planned action or objective. The calculation of the benefit is determined by the adversary and is difficult if not impossible to accurately assess by coercing nations.[44] Things such as nationalism, religion, ideology and economics are just a few of the things that can influence a nation's benefit decision. For one nation to assume or forecast the value another nation places on this benefit calculation is difficult due to cultural and other differences, but the estimation provides a basis for coercion. Though benefits are not usually directly manipulatable by the coercer, the benefits are impacted by decreasing the probability of gain or increasing the cost or probability of cost to the adversary.[45]

Costs are what the adversary nation expects or anticipates paying in order to gain the objective or action.[46] The ability to bear the expected costs and whether the adversary actually believes these costs will occur directly affect decision-making. Ultimately, a rational decision maker would assume that when the costs exceed the expected benefits, the adversary would concede to coercion.[47] Therefore, to coerce the adversary the coercing nation must be willing to escalate the threat in the event the adversary believes the expected benefit worth the threatened cost. It is also important to

---

[42] Schelling, 78-79; Byman and Waxman, 10-12; Pape, 15-18; Johnson, Mueller, and Taft, 25.

[43] Byman and Waxman, 11.

[44] Ibid., 11.

[45] Pape, 16.

[46] Byman and Waxman, 11.

[47] Pape, 16.

remember that costs are not necessarily monetary or property costs, as things such as domestic political power or national pride also enter the decision calculus of the adversary. Simply threatening costs are not enough, as the adversary must believe the threat probable.

Probabilities of the threatened costs or of the expected gains are also necessary for the adversary to analyze in making their decision. If the adversary believes it is more probable that the benefits will outweigh the cost, they will likely resist. Conversely, if the probable costs are greater than the gain, or the adversary believes acquiring the gain improbable, the adversary will likely concede.[48] Ultimately, the difficulty in analyzing and estimating the coercee's benefit calculus as well as their perceptions of benefit and cost make cultural study and awareness helpful, though it will not ensure success at predicting what the adversary thinks. What the adversary believes, or his perception, is closely linked to the probability calculus.

The adversary has to take account of the situation and surrounding factors to determine what it perceives to be true. Coercion attempts to manipulate what the adversary believes or perceives; therefore, this perception is key. "These perceived costs and benefits are products of the magnitude of the dangers and profits the adversary sees ahead for a given path and the probability of their occurrence."[49] Ultimately, if the adversary believes his gains outweigh the costs or thinks the coercer's threats are not probable; concession is not likely to occur. Robert Pape provides the following model to demonstrate the cost-benefit assessment:

$$R = B \, p(B) - C \, p(C)$$

---

[48] Ibid., 17.

[49] Byman and Waxman, 11.

Where R=value of resistance; B=potential benefits of resistance; p(B)=probability of attaining benefits by continued resistance; C=costs of resistance; and p(C)=probability of suffering costs.[50] The coercee will concede if R< 0, so the coercer will threaten punishment to increase cost of resistance or raise the coercee's risk of increased cost, or use denial threats to reduce the probability that continued resistance will yield benefits for the coercee.[51] Essentially, the coercer attempts to manipulate the formula by making the adversary believe the real or perceived costs exceed any gains or that the probability of adversary gains are too low to continue to resist coercer demands. To succeed in coercion, these threats of punishment or denial must be consistently stated and backed with credible and capable elements of power. In context of the coercer's demands, threats and the adversary's own determination, the decision to acquiesce or bear the cost of noncompliance must ultimately be made by the coercee. Though this decision rests with the coercee, the coercer determines how to proceed by defining the objective.

Objective

An essential element in coercion strategy is determining the intended objective. What is the issue at stake driving the country's involvement in the conflict? Is it to defend a vital interest, to defend an ally, protect access to resources, defend values, promote stability? While there are any number of potential interests, the decision to be made is whether the level of interest rises to the point that the use of force, or threatened use of force, will be applied.[52] In making this determination, an often used method of

---

[50] Pape, 15-18.

[51] Ibid., 17-18.

[52] As discussed earlier, other elements of national power are also capable of applying pressure, but this paper focuses on application or threat of military force. For further discussion of coercion with other instruments of national power see Joseph Nye, *Soft Power*, New York: Public Affairs, 2004; also George and Simons, *Limits of Coercive Diplomacy*.

formulating strategy is ends-ways-means, whereby the end (objective) is determined, driving the way (leadership decapitation, sanctions, damage infrastructure, etc.) and using the means (one or more instruments of national power).[53] Once the US objective is determined, the President will apply elements of national power to influence the outcome.

Objectives vary depending upon the situation, including the national interests involved, involvement of allies and the like. Therefore, no specific list of events can be scripted to determine when or if military power will be used. According to Henry Kissinger, "A clear definition of the national interest needs to be an equally essential guide to American policy."[54] In that light, Presidents have published their idea of national interests in their respective National Security Strategies. These interests are set forth to inform national and international audiences of US interests, but are not specific to the ways or means the nation may use to further or protect them. Explaining these interests in open forum and applying their defense consistently contribute directly to the essential elements of credibility and capability.

Credibility

In order to influence an adversary to change behavior or action, the coercer's threats must be believed or the adversary will perceive staying the course is acceptable and possibly even effective. Most important in persuading the adversary of the coercer's strength of purpose is to state the intended objective with clarity and consistency.[55] First, if the adversary is expected to comply with a demand, the expectation must be known and understood. Second, the objective demand must be consistent in relating to the adversary

---

[53] Byman and Waxman, 27; Henry C. Bartlett, G. Paul Holmann and Timothy E. Somes, *The Art and Strategy of Force Planning* (Newport: Naval War College Press, 2004), 18-22.

[54] Henry Kissinger, *Diplomacy* (New York: Simon and Schuster, 1994), 811.

[55] George and Simons, 280.

the exact expectation and consequences for noncompliance. Changing objectives during the coercion attempt can lead to confusion and also make the adversary doubt the will or strength of the coercer's commitment to the demand. The coercion attempt in Panama discussed in chapter three provides an example, where changing US objectives led Noriega to perceive the demand was not serious. As Byman and Waxman make very clear, "Will and credibility matter as much as, and often more than, the overall balance of forces."[56] No force is credible if the coercer appears unwilling to commit the force.

Other items can affect the credibility of the coercer such as coalitions, public support, and amount of pain the adversary can accept. Many items such as these must be taken into account when determining what threats to issue while maintaining credibility. Coalitions can bolster the coercer's credibility if in agreement; however, diverging interests may dilute resolve and call credibility into question.[57] The coercer can emphasize the ability to strike with precision; however, that same reliance on precision may also eliminate the ability to threaten freely as collateral damage or perceived injury to civilians becomes less accepted by allies and domestic compatriots.[58] While the threat of greater punishment is intended to coerce, a point can be reached when credibility is reduced as the coercer's capability is politically constrained.[59] Retaliatory strikes may also factor into decision-making; however, the coercer's ability to accept retaliation punishment need not be a factor in credibility so long as the adversary believes he will suffer the threat.[60] As evident, credibility is maintained by threatening the adversary

---

[56] Byman and Waxman, 18.

[57] Ibid., 240.

[58] Ibid., 233.

[59] Pape, 28.

[60] Schelling, 36.

enough to raise the cost to be greater than the expected gain without crossing the threshold of believability or losing support from the domestic and international audience. As with credibility, the capability to apply the threatened pressure is also essential.

Capability

In order for a nation to successfully coerce another nation, the coercee must believe the coercer has, along with the will to use, the tools that make the threat. As previously discussed, the coercee has to make a calculated cost benefit calculation in order to make a decision. If the coercer provides signals that indicate hesitancy in action, the coercee is more likely to resist coercion. Making statements such as, "we will not use ground troops" or "we will not bomb infrastructure" or "we will only be involved a matter of days" indicates a lack of will or commitment and can result in coercion failure. Along the same line, the type of coercive instrument used depends upon the perceived effectiveness, coercer cost, and overall political context that determines the level of force desired.[61] The wrong choice, like making limiting statements, can be counterproductive. For the best chance of coercion success, the coercer must use consistent statements combined with capable instruments of national power aimed at the coercee's most vulnerable points. These points will vary, but the coercer must continue to add pressure on these points until reaching escalation dominance.

Escalation Dominance

According to Byman and Waxman, "escalation dominance is the ability to increase the threatened cost to an adversary while denying the adversary the opportunity

---

[61] Byman and Waxman, 87.

to neutralize those costs or to counter escalate."[62] Essentially, the coercer issues a threat,

which can be from any form of national power such as diplomatic, economic, or military

force. In return, the coercee is then given a decision to either acquiesce to the demand or

resist. If the coercee resists, the coercer can give up or add additional pressure through

force or sanctions, depending on the coercive instruments being used. This back and

forth continues until one side gives in or the situation progresses to actual war, where the

winning side makes the loser acquiesce through military force. Coercion is difficult to

achieve as it requires the coercer to initiate threats and be willing to initiate hostilities if

required.[63] Therefore, before deciding to use coercion to force a nation to comply with

demands or change behavior, the coercing nation must determine the objective, maintain

consistency in the demand, and keep all coercive instrument options open. Used

effectively, coercion can be a valuable component of foreign policy.

Value of Coercion

As pointed out by Alexander George and William Simons, coercion offers the

chance to achieve reasonable objectives with less cost, minimum or no bloodshed, and

fewer political or psychological costs.[64] Coercion also offers the coercing nation the

opportunity to show action toward resolving an issue while taking time to allow the

adversary opportunities to affect the outcome. Coercion is more appealing than brute

military force as it shows willingness to work and compromise with others rather than

simply resorting to war. However, to show coercion's effectiveness, the coercer needs to

measure success.

---

[62] Ibid., 30.

[63] Pape, 6.

[64] George and Simons, 9.

23

Measuring Success

Coercion can be difficult to measure as results can be interpreted differently. Was the coercion successful if the objective is achieved even if the threatened forcing function had to be applied? Was coercion successful if the coercer modified the demanded objectives in negotiation to achieve less than the original demand? Coercion success or failure is difficult to measure in binary terms, as coercion does not always lead to simple yes or no answers.[65] Understanding what the coercer actually desires, the coercer's goals as well as the coercee's goals each influence the success or failure grading.[66] Ultimately, success or failure will be determined relative to the context of each situation, realizing competing goals, methods and third party actors may affect the eventual outcome. In that light, one has to view the coercion attempt by looking at the desired outcome as stated by national leaders, compared to the actual outcome achieved. In the case studies covered later, success or failure of coercion is graded through consistency of a clear message by the coercer, credible expectation of the use of threatened military power and the belief a capable military force would be employed.

Coercion in US Foreign Policy

The US has often used coercion to get other nations to change behavior. The methods of coercion used vary, but usually begin with diplomatic and economic pressures, then advance to threats of force. There are often debates on when and why the use of force is necessary; however, US Presidents have not been prevented from using coercive force by Congress or the people when they desired to use force. In a study conducted by James Meernik, US Presidents from Truman to Clinton, 1948 to 1998, have

---

[65] Byman and Waxman, 35.

[66] Ibid., 34.

used military force an average of 52.5 percent of the time when confronted with opportunities to use force.[67] His study found in 605 crises, force was used 318 times. Each President since 1998 has also used coercion in foreign policy, making evident the need to understand how best to apply the elements of national power to achieve success.

Imposed Limitations

Limitations are often imposed upon the elements of power employed in coercion. The problem, however, is not in imposing limitations on the levels, types, or duration of force used. The problem in coercion can arise when these limitations are publicly declared, which can make the coercee assume the level of commitment to the objective is low. Low commitment lends to low credibility and encourages the adversary to counter the coercion or simply wait out the US, believing his own commitment is stronger. Restrictions on the types of force used also reduce the capability of the force, as countering threats in a single domain are much easier. In the end, this commitment, capability and credibility issue can raise the costs of coercion, if the commitment and credibility on the use of force are carried through to achieving objectives.

Reasons for Use of Force

The threatened or actual use of force is used when national leadership feels strongly about the objective. People often argue that military force should only be used in the case of vital interests of the US or its allies, such as survival. Others argue important interests also justify the need for the use of force, and still others believe the furthering of democratic ideals and preservation of humanitarian rights also rise to the level of defense or intervention with force. Presidents set policy and provide guidance

---

[67] James D. Meernik, *The Political Use of Military Force in US Foreign Policy* (Burlington: Ashgate Publishing Company, 2004), 15-16.

through speeches and documents that allude to when they intend to back policy with force. The next chapter discusses how several senior US officials proposed the nation should use military force, followed by thoughts promulgated by Presidents Bush, Clinton and Obama, who were in charge during the coercion case studies discussed later.

CHAPTER 2: US MILITARY POWER IN COERCION

The use of United States (US) military power is often a contentious issue. Using military force to coerce the behavior of an adversary not a direct "threat" to the nation is even more problematic, as people differ on when or how force should be used. Problems arise when objectives are ill-defined or the level of interest thought too low for military force. Eager to show action despite ill-defined objectives or interests, leaders will often provide force-limiting statements to try to minimize the appearance of force in coercion. Several political and military leaders have attempted to provide doctrine on the use of force to allow, when necessary, credible and successful application without undue limits. This makes the decision regarding interests, objectives, and if force is required when considering options to resolve a conflict or crisis.

According to Clausewitz, "the political object is the goal, war is the means of reaching it, and means can never be considered in isolation from their purpose."[1] He goes on to say that war is a paradoxical trinity, consisting of the people, the commander and his army, and the government; with political aims being the business of the government alone.[2] In a democracy, while we place trust in the government to defend the nation, the people demand a continued influence on policy, especially a policy to use military force of which they are part. The framers of the US Constitution made this point clear by granting the Congress, the body closest to the people, the power to declare war and sustain financing of the military and military action. However, the President, as

---

[1] Carl von Clausewitz, *On War*, ed. and trans. Michael Howard and Peter Paret (Princeton: Princeton University Press, 1976), 99.

[2] Ibid., 101.

commander-in-chief, often uses military force to implement foreign policy including some uses with limited consultation with Congress.

When and how to use military force, short of declared war, to execute foreign policy remains a continuing debate among military and civilian leaders alike. Since World War II, "US interests have moved from being defensive and reactive in nature to offensive and proactive in nature."[3] This became reality due to the threat posed by the formation of the Soviet Union and the resultant Cold War. "The global struggle with the Soviet Union and communism led to a foreign policy based on zero-sum game assumptions. Since any gain for the Soviet Union meant an equivalent loss for the US, US interests, whether real or reputational, were perceived at stake everywhere."[4] In this context, the US participated in a conflict in Vietnam which continues to influence the decision of when and how to use force today. The war in Vietnam is not a topic for this paper, but the effort to thwart communist expansion there led to a protracted conflict that was ultimately unpopular domestically and failed to achieve the intended purpose. According to Admiral US Grant Sharp, former Commander-in-Chief, Pacific, 1964-1968, America's involvement in Vietnam was a debacle and the first time America lost a war.[5]

The US loss in the Vietnam conflict, or at least not achieving the objective of an independent South Vietnam, many people have researched the conflict to learn lessons that would help prevent future failure. Many lessons can be drawn from such a long conflict, but some participating and future leaders felt key failures occurred that should be remembered. Admiral Sharp believed civilian leaders conducted "a flagrant misuse of

---

[3] James D. Meernik, *The Political Use of Military Force in US Foreign Policy* (Burlington: Ashgate Publishing Company, 2004), 74.

[4] Ibid., 64.

[5] US Grant Sharp, *Strategy for Defeat: Vietnam in Restrospect* (Novato: Presidio Press, 1986), 89.

airpower"[6] and a "fatal lack of will surfaced at the highest level of our government."[7]

Sharp also noted several Defense Department civilians insisted on limiting air and naval

power in exchange for a broadened ground war, despite objections from the Joint Chiefs

of Staff (JCS) and civilians within the State Department.[8] General Westmoreland, US

military commander in Vietnam, indicated President Johnson bowed to wishful-thinking

theorists and naïve Administration officials to order bombing pauses, a decision he

believed ill informed and folly.[9] He went on to say, "It was a mistake to permit

appointive civilian officials, lacking military experience and knowledge of military

history and oblivious to the lessons of the Communist diplomatic machinations, to wield

undue influence in the decision-making process."[10] Caspar Weinberger, Secretary of

Defense from 1981-87, said "The war in Vietnam, with our 'limited objectives' and yet

unlimited willingness to commit troops reinforced my belief it was a terrible mistake for

a government to commit soldiers to battle without any intention of supporting them

sufficiently to win, and indeed without any intention of winning."[11] And finally, General

Colin Powell, National Security Advisor from 1987-88 and Chairman of the Joint Chiefs

of Staff (CJCS) from 1988-92, said, "If the Vietnam war had taught one inelectable

---

[6] Sharp, 90.

[7] Ibid., 100.

[8] Ibid., 107-110.

[9] General William Westmoreland, *A Soldier Reports* (Garden City: Doubleday & Co. Inc., 1976), 144.

[10] Ibid., 145.

[11] Caspar Weinberger, *Fighting for Peace: Seven Critical Years in the Pentagon* (New York: Warner Books, 1990), 8-9.

lesson, it was that when political objectives become muddy and politicians become generals, the cause is lost."[12]

Coming out of the Vietnam conflict, the nation mourned the loss of nearly 60,000 service members killed and the belief the Administration had misled the need for and level of involvement in Vietnam. Congress attempted to restrain the Executive Branch use of military force with the War Powers Act of 1973, the draft ended and the military sought to rebuild the force.[13] These events shaped the thinking of our leaders throughout the 1980s and 1990s, sparking much debate on when, where and how to apply US military force short of war. Doctrine flowed from this debate, primarily centering on the perception of "all or nothing" or "limited objective" strategies.

Doctrine

Doctrine on the use of force for political purposes, short of declared war, was introduced in the 1980s beginning with Secretary of Defense Caspar Weinberger. He felt strongly regarding proposed use of force in situations being faced by the US and opposed many other government officials. Weinberger's views, later added to by General Colin Powell, established the doctrine sometimes referred to as an "all or nothing" use of force. Many believe this approach too strict, unduly limiting options the President needs to face foreign policy crises, and countered this doctrine. These views, supported by Secretaries of State George Shultz and Madeline Albright, as well as Secretary of Defense Les Aspin, are presented in the section of limited objectives.

---

[12] Howard Means, *Colin Powell: Soldier/Statesman-Statesman/Soldier* (New York: Donald I.Fine, Inc., 1992), 5.

[13] Library of Congress. "War Powers Resolution," Law Library of Congress, http://loc.gov/law/help/war-powers.pht (accessed March 21, 2012) and Chuck Raasch, "Veterans in Congress, US on the Decline Since End of the Draft," *Deseret News*, May 30, 2010.

All or Nothing

Secretary Weinberger was not against having a strong defense nor against using military force to properly defend the US or its vital interests. In his book, *Fighting for Peace: Seven Critical Years in the Pentagon*, he said, "it is an extremely risky and dangerous business for any country to allow itself to become unarmed and unready for war."[14] He understood the need for a strong defense but also realized defense expenditures are never popular in a democracy.[15] These thoughts are important because the Reagan Administration, which he was part of, had embarked on an ambitious plan to increase military capacity. He states, "our strategy was to convince our friends to stay closely allied with us and to convince the Soviets they could not win any war they might start with us or our allies."[16] This military buildup is widely accepted to have aided in the demise and breakup of the Soviet Union, resulting in an end to the Cold War in 1989.

In light of the ongoing military buildup, members of the State Department and National Security Council (NSC) staff began suggesting troop deployments to support foreign policy objectives, such as deploying US Marines as peace observers in Lebanon. Some of these missions were opposed by Secretary Weinberger for different reasons, although they brought him back to lessons learned from the Vietnam conflict. Early on, then-Secretary of State Alexander Haig suggested "we would have to invade Cuba to put an end to the Castro regime."[17] To this, Weinberger was convinced in order to go to war, the American public must be convinced that US national interests demanded the need to

---

[14] Weinberger, 8.

[15] Ibid., 67.

[16] Ibid., 79.

[17] Ibid., 31.

go to war. While this action was only discussed and not used, other foreign policy concerns arose that did involve military employment.

The State Department, led by Secretary George Shultz, and the NSC staff wanted to use military force in Lebanon and Central America in 1983-84.[18] Secretary Weinberger and military leaders opposed using force in these situations because they believed support of the people was lacking and the objectives were ill defined. Additionally, they were concerned over indiscriminate use of military force in diplomatic efforts, which would invariably lead to irresolvable and unpopular conflicts.[19] Ultimately, troops were deployed to Lebanon as part of a Multinational Force (MNF), which resulted in 241 US service members killed and 112 wounded in a suicide bombing of the barracks in Beirut, Lebanon.[20] The tragic loss of life and a lack of clear objective led President Reagan to withdraw the forces. Regarding the deployment to Lebanon, Secretary Weinberger stated, "I objected very strongly because the MNF would not have any mission that could be defined."[21] The JCS opposed because without a clearly defined objective, determining the size, armament and rules of engagement were difficult at best.

As a result of the loss of lives in Lebanon and in effort to prevent further use of military force in perceived inappropriate ways, Secretary Weinberger created a list of six principal tests to determine when the US should apply military force. He unveiled this

---

[18] Michael I. Handel, *Masters of War: Classical Strategic Thought, Third Edition* (Portland: Frank Cass Publishers, 2001), 307.

[19] Ibid., 310.

[20] Department of Defense. *Report of the DoD Commission on Beirut International Airport Terrorist Attack, 23 Oct 1983*, by Admiral (Ret) Robert L. Long. Department of Defense. Washington D.C., November 1983.

[21] Weinberger, 151.

list at a speech to the National Press Club on November 28, 1984, summarized as follows:[22]

> 1. The United States should not commit forces to combat overseas unless the interest is vital to the US or its allies. He clarifies, "That emphatically does not mean that we should declare beforehand, as we did with Korea in 1950 that an area is outside our strategic perimeter."

> 2. If the decision is made to commit troops, the US should do so wholeheartedly, and with clear intention of winning. Realizing if only limited force is required to win objectives, then we should not hesitate to commit forces that are sized accordingly.

> 3. We should have clearly defined political and military objectives if we decide to commit forces. We should also know precisely how our forces can accomplish those clearly defined objectives. Again Weinberger clarifies, "Don't assign a combat mission to a force configured for peacekeeping."

> 4. The relationship between our objectives and the force committed - their size, composition, disposition - must be continually reassessed and adjusted if necessary. Continue to ask, "Is this conflict in our national interest?"

> 5. There must be some reasonable assurance we will have the support of the American people and their elected representatives in Congress. "Don't ask troops not to win, but just be there."

> 6. Commitment of US forces to combat should be as a last resort.

According to Secretary Weinberger, "these tests can help us avoid being drawn inexorably into an endless morass, where it is not vital to our national interests to fight."[23] Weinberger remained concerned that military force would be used rather than exercising diplomacy and other elements of national power. He said, "The NSC staff, with no responsibility for the safety and well-being of our troops, were always eager to use the military for political or 'diplomatic' purposes whenever that filled their personal agendas."[24] While not providing specific prescriptions for when force can be used, the

---

[22] Ibid., 441-443.

[23] Ibid., 444.

[24] Ibid., 361.

Weinberger Doctrine was and remains a clear, objective approach to determining the need to use military force short of war. The Weinberger Doctrine has made and will continue to make an important contribution to US national security policy.[25] Although valuable, the Weinberger Doctrine has been modified over time or not used.

General Colin Powell also became a senior leader, in both military and civilian positions, heavily influenced by the conflict in Vietnam. After serving two tours of duty in that conflict and progressing through the ranks within the US Army, Powell had clear ideas of how military force should be used. As Weinberger advocated a clear intent to win, Powell said, "Decisive means are always to be preferred, even if they are not always possible. So you bet I get nervous when so-called experts suggest all we need is a little surgical bombing or a limited attack. When the desired result is not achieved, a new set of experts then comes forward with talk of a little escalation."[26] The limited means and escalation he speaks to are clear methods employed by the Kennedy and Johnson Administrations during Vietnam. History of this conflict provided examples of unclear objectives, limited means of military employment without well thought out purpose, and poor overall strategy. On objectives, Powell said, "have a clear political objective and once you have one make sure you have the right statement of strategic military objectives to achieve the political objectives and that you put the resources to bear on it."[27] As a senior leader, General Powell wanted to make sure military force stood the best chance of success when employed in future conflicts.

---

[25] Handel, 324.

[26] David Roth, *Sacred Honor: Colin Powell, the Inside Account of His Life and Triumphs* (Grand Rapids: Zondervan Publishing House, 1993), 247.

[27] Means, 273.

General Powell was a military assistant to Secretary Weinberger in 1983, appointed as Deputy and later the National Security Advisor (NSA) in 1987, and then served as the Chairman, Joint Chiefs of Staff.[28] As military assistant, Powell had seen the Weinberger speech prior to release and appeared to think in similar terms. Powell has said, "What makes generals nervous is when objectives are not clear and the military does not know what it is getting into. If force is used imprecisely or out of frustration rather than clear analysis, the situation can be made worse."[29] As the Deputy NSA, General Powell commented on how the NSC was paralyzed by Secretary Shultz's advocacy of military solutions while Secretary Weinberger preferred diplomatic solutions.[30] Powell understood that experts can disagree on the use of force and remained convinced that taking time for this debate was essential even as he agreed military force should be used as a last resort, rather than prior to working diplomatic solutions.

Secretary Weinberger resigned in 1987 and was replaced as Secretary of Defense by Frank Carlucci. As NSA, Powell sided with Carlucci and then CJCS Admiral Crowe against State Department advocacy of force to overthrow Panamanian Dictator Manuel Noriega in Panama.[31] They believed that using military force was not appropriate to resolve the situation at the time, resulting in continued diplomacy and pressure by other means. Powell learned that in Vietnam you could not assume military force can accomplish any objective. Sometimes military force only gets you into a situation that

---

[28] Roth, 127, 190.

[29] Ibid., 246-247.

[30] Means, 233.

[31] Ibid., 248.

perhaps you cannot get out of.[32] These experiences would serve him advising the President and Secretary of Defense in his next position as well.

As CJCS, General Powell advised the President and Secretary of Defense on conflicts in Panama, Iraq (Operation DESERT STORM), Somalia and Bosnia. In each of these conflicts, General Powell's advice remained consistent even when he was opposed by other senior government officials. As previously shown, Powell insisted on the need for clear political and military objectives, that military force should be used in an overwhelmingly decisive fashion, have reasonable assumption of public support and used only as a last resort. Additionally, he felt military operations should have limited time spans and not be open-ended, which was an additional requirement Weinberger had not specified in his speech. According to Powell, "You simply have to have buried deep in your psyche the fact that American people are not that patient if conducting a military operation, try to do it in a way that gets it over quickly."[33] He understood that clear objectives, overwhelming force, popular support and meaningful progress toward objectives were keys to success. In Panama, covered in the case studies later, and Iraq, his advice as CJCS was generally followed. In Somalia, there were many changes to objectives, timelines and forces used that ran counter to his doctrine with the operation ending poorly. For Bosnia, another conflict covered in the case studies section, he recommended against involvement in military force until his retirement. Powell's advice was clear and relatively uncomplicated, "if we choose an offensive option, we must have decisive force or risk terrible consequences."[34]

---

[32] Ibid., 264.

[33] Ibid., 273.

[34] Roth, 196.

Although the Weinberger and Powell Doctrines appear logical, they are not prescriptive for every situation. Many critics emerged to argue against these tests to enable use of force, arguing the tests made the use of force by the US nearly impossible. These opposing ideas are covered under the term-limited objectives.

Limited Objectives

Several high-level US government officials argued against the stringent use of force requirements outlined by Weinberger and Powell. Among them include Secretaries of State Shultz, Christopher and Albright, as well as Chairman of the House Armed Services Committee and, later, Secretary of Defense Les Aspin. Each of their arguments will be covered in the following paragraphs.

Secretary Shultz argued for the use of force on several occasions when the decision to use force would not pass the Weinberger test. In particular, Shultz took exception with the notions of only using force for vital interests, using force as a last resort, insisting on public support, and stipulating timelines. In addressing the United Nations (UN) in 1982, Shultz said, "America's yearning for peace does not lead us to be hesitant in developing our strength or using it when necessary."[35] While Secretary of State, he advocated use of force in Lebanon, Central America, Grenada, Libya and Panama in effort to coerce those countries to behave in a fashion acceptable to the US. According to Shultz, the important element to work for is legitimacy for what you are doing, not just legality.[36]

---

[35] George Shultz, "US Foreign Policy: Realism and Progress," *Vital Speeches of the Day* 49, no. 4 (December 1, 1982): 99.

[36] Federal News Service, "Salon Luncheon with Former Secretary of State George Shultz, 29 October 2009," Carnegie Endowment for International Peace, http://carnegieendowment.org/files/1027carnegie-shultz (accessed 21 January 2012).

Contrary to using vital interests as a requirement for use of force, there are instances where moral and ethical choices drive a nation to intervene in order to prevent unjust events. Having the willingness to defend those beliefs and values make the nation's actions consistent and legitimate in the free world. Shultz was clear to point out that inaction by a nation carries consequences just as taking action.[37] Insisting on use of force as a last resort is also problematic, especially if the need to use force involves defending the homeland or a vital interest. Action may have to be taken immediately in order to deter, signal resolve or even preempt the actions of others in order to defend properly.[38] In addition to the potential need to respond prior to last resort, Shultz also understood taking action would not always be popular because there are never guarantees of public support in advance of a conflict.[39] There are occasions when leadership may not be able to notify the public in advance. At other times, leadership may make the unpopular decision to use force, understanding future work may be required to obtain the public and domestic political support to continue the effort. Finally, stipulating timelines for the use of force can signal a lack of will or effort. Regarding the Obama Administration, Shultz wrote, "How can you say that if I haven't won by six or nine months from now, I'm leaving?"[40] Signaling the limits of US commitment in advance surely encourages an adversary to buy time, waiting for terms favorable to their cause.

Secretaries of State Albright and Christopher also believed there are times the US needs to use military force to coerce an adversary even when not passing the Weinberger

---

[37] Handel, 321.

[38] Ibid., 319.

[39] Ibid., 319.

[40] Ben Birnbaum, "Shultz to Obama: You're Out of Your Mind," *The Washington Times*, October 4, 2010.

and Powell tests, such as requiring a vital interest, timeline, or having a clearly defined mission. On foreign policy, Secretary Albright wrote, "To protect our interests, we must take action, forge agreements, build institutions and provide an example to bring the world together around the basic principles of democracy, open markets, law and commitment to peace."[41] This idea posits that creating an open, stable, free-market and democratic world better maintains peace and protects US interests over time. In speeches, Albright urges audiences to support American involvement in the world and not become "ditherers or neoprotectionists" who fail to act when action is needed to forge alliances, deter aggression and keep the peace.[42] This reasoning advocates action, often with military force, to coerce the behavior of nations or groups in order to advance US morals and ideals to obtain the desired environment. While US Ambassador to the U.N., prior to becoming Secretary of State, Albright heartily advocated the use of force in Bosnia counter to Powell, who felt the cost too high for this open-ended conflict that was not a vital interest. At an NSC meeting, Albright asked Powell, "What are you saving this superb military for, Colin, if we can't use it?"[43] Her desire to use force in Bosnia and later in Kosovo to stop violence against Muslim peoples also provides examples of her willingness to use military power for what she considered moral purposes. Additionally, both of these conflicts lacked clear political objectives and also expected timelines. Albright said, "We get involved where the crime is huge, where it affects our stability, or where there is an organization capable of handling it. There is not a doctrine

---

[41] Thomas W. Lippman, *Madeline Albright and the New American Diplomacy* (Boulder: Westview Press, 2002), 315.

[42] Ibid., 97.

[43] Madeline Albright with Bob Woodward, *Madam Secretary* (New York: Miramax Books, 2003), 182.

that really sets this forth in an organized way yet."[44] For his part, Secretary Christopher cited the Administration's pillars of building America's prosperity, modernizing America's military, and promoting human rights and democracy abroad as the foreign policy to confront the post-Cold War challenges.[45] He advocated the use of air strikes against the Serbians in Bosnia, hoping this action would compel the Serbians to acquiesce. When travelling to Europe to push this agenda, the plan received luke-warm support and led President Clinton to be uncomfortable with the proposal.[46]

Secretary Les Aspin was somewhat less activist in his approach but also disagreed with the Powell Doctrine. In October 1992, Aspin castigated the idea of an "all or nothing" approach as being too restrictive. Aspin favored being flexible and using the military as a precision tool to achieve limited objectives.[47] While Aspin is not unique in advocating for limited objectives, the notion of using the military as a precision tool brings back poor experiences from the Vietnam conflict when civilian leaders directed tactical military actions to create results they desired, ignoring the expert military advice of professionals. As has been stated before, "civilians are often more interested in using small doses of force to accomplish good deeds, such as peacekeeping or discipline of odious regimes abroad, or they wish to show that force can be used economically, without wasteful overkill."[48] Ultimately, the officials pushing for the limited objective approach tended to believe in the requirement for the US to use its instruments of power

---

[44] Lippman, 318

[45] Ibid., 314.

[46] Nigel Hamilton, *Bill Clinton: Mastering the Presidency* (New York: Persius Books Group, 2007), 127.

[47] Roth, 247.

[48] Richard K. Betts, "Are Civil-Military Relations Still a Problem?" In *American Civil-Military Relations: The Soldier and the State in a New Era* (Baltimore: The Johns Hopkins University Press, 2009), 15.

in order to advance ideals throughout the world. As such, the military option is often used in order to resolve the situation or crises in the most expedient manner. Making actors around the globe understand the US has, and will consistently use, a strong military is thought to make the diplomatic instrument of national power more effective. As Secretary Schulz told the UN in his 1982 speech, "The bulwark of America's strength is military power for peace."[49] Unfortunately, if the objective is not clear or the end ill-defined, the military can be embroiled in an endless action or coercion can fail.

Policy

Presidents communicate their national security policies in many ways, including speeches, directives and strategy documents. Each Administration provides themes addressing how they intend to use military force to defend the nation and its interests. The following sections highlight the policies advanced by the George H.W. Bush, William J. Clinton, and Barak H. Obama Administrations, which were in office during the conflicts presented later in the case studies. Knowing how these leaders intended to use force aids to understanding how and why each applied force for coercion.

President George H.W. Bush

President George H.W. Bush was Vice President under President Reagan for eight years when America used military power to defend interests abroad, indicating his strength of purpose. In his inaugural address, President Bush said, "We know how to secure a more just and prosperous life for man on Earth: through free markets, free speech, free elections, and the exercise of free will unhampered by the state."[50] He went

---

[49] Shultz, 99.

[50] George Bush Presidential Library, "Inaugural Address, January 20, 1989," http://bushlibrary.tamu.edu/research/public_papers.php?id=1356&year=1989&month=all (accessed January 21, 2012).

on to show his desire to engage in the world and continue peaceful advancement by saying America offers new engagement, staying strong for peace. Following the military action taken against Panamanian dictator Noriega, President Bush addressed the nation and stated he looked forward to strengthening relations with democracies in this hemisphere.[51] President Bush clearly described his desire to promote American values abroad. Finally, in his 1991 State of the Union address, he stated, "the cause of peace must be served by an America strong enough and sure enough to defend our interests and our ideals."[52]

President William J. Clinton

President Clinton began his era with a speech in December 1991, stating his desire to put promoting freedom, democracy and economic growth over stability.[53] He went on to state America needs to lead the world in promoting these values by shaping the environment to encourage the spread of democracy. In his inaugural address in January 1993 he said, "When our vital interests are challenged or the will and conscience of the international community is defied, we will act, with peaceful diplomacy whenever possible, with force when necessary."[54] In 1994, President Clinton signed Presidential Decision Directive 25, stating how US forces will conduct peacekeeping operations to "support the full range of activities from preventive diplomacy through peacekeeping to

---

[51] George Bush Presidential Library, "White House address, December 20, 1989," http://bushlibrary.tamu.edu/research/public_papers.php?id=1356&year=1989&month=all (accessed January 21, 2012).

[52] George Bush Presidential Library, "State of the Union, January 20, 1991," http://bushlibrary.tamu.edu/research/public_papers.php?id=1356&year=1989&month=all (accessed January 21, 2012).

[53] Democratic Leadership Council, "A New Covenant for American Security: address at Georgetown University," http://www.dlc.org/ndol_ci.cfm?kaid=128&subid=174&contentid=250537 (accessed January 15, 2012).

[54] Shirley A. Warshaw, *Presidential Profiles: The Clinton Years* (New York: Facts On File, Inc., 2004), 369.

peace enforcement."[55] These thoughts were put into action as the US became involved in the conflicts in Bosnia and Kosovo discussed in the next chapter. He continued in his 1995 State of the Union address, "Our security depends upon our continued world leadership for peace and freedom and democracy."[56] Clinton continued to show the desire to shape the world in line with US ideals and values, believing this would make the world safer for all. Finally, in 2000, President Clinton states, "We can't prevent every conflict and stop every outrage, but where our interests are at stake and when we can make a difference, we should be, and must be, peacemakers."[57]

President Barak H. Obama

President Obama began presenting his foreign policy with speeches made during the election campaign, stating clearly how he would employ military force. In Denver, on 28 August 2008, he said, "As Commander-in-Chief, I will never hesitate to defend the nation, but I will only send troops into harm's way with a clear mission and a sacred commitment to give them the equipment they need in battle."[58] This statement laid out his intent to always provide a clear political objective and properly equip the force to successfully accomplish that objective. In a National Security Speech in May 2009, President Obama stated, "Time and again, our values have been our best national security

---

[55] William J. Clinton Presidential Library, "PDD/NSC-25: US Policy on Reforming Multilateral Peace Operations," Clinton Presidential Library. http://www.clintonlibrary.gov/_previous/Documents/2010%20FOIA/Presidential%20Directives/PDD-25.pdf (accessed January 15, 2012).

[56] Warshaw, 410.

[57] Ibid, 418.

[58] Mary Frances Berry and Josh Gottheimer, *Power in Words: The Stories Behind Barak Obama's Speeches, from the State House to the White House* (Boston: Beacon Books, 2010), 241.

asset–in war and peace; in times of ease and in eras of upheaval."[59] This statement made clear the intent to stand by and promote our values of freedom and democracy in the world fraught with instability. The notion of spreading idealism in foreign policy would continue. Finally, on 27 May 2010, a White House press release supporting the 2010 National Security Strategy stated the Administration's foreign policy is driven by the themes of security, prosperity, values and international order.[60] As described in the news release under peacekeeping and armed conflict, President Obama is the first US president to meet with leading UN troop-contributing nations to obtain their inputs on policies that will strengthen peacekeeper performance worldwide. This indicates the President is willing to use US military power to support peacekeeping missions in conjunction with the UN, implying direct US national interests may not be required for the use of force to advance foreign policy.

The next section will review four cases of coercion attempts during the above administrations, providing a better understanding of the how these political leaders intended to use military force. Each case provides examples that inform how future coercion can be better implemented.

---

[59] The White House, "Remarks by the President on National Security," National Archives, http://www.whitehouse.gov/the_press_office/Remarks-by-the-President-On-National-Security-5-21-09 (accessed August 19, 2011).

[60] The White House, "Advancing Our Interests: Actions in Support of the President's NSS," Office of the Press Secretary, http://www.whitehouse.gov/the-press-office/advancing-our-interests-actions-support-presidents-national-security-strategy (accessed August 19, 2011).

CHAPTER 3: CASE STUDIES

Studying historical cases provides the ability to learn from past actions to improve future actions. In this chapter, four United States (US) coercion attempts provide a venue to examine coercion within the context of the existing post-Cold War international environment. In each case, the US attempted to coerce other nations using threats of military power as one of the forcing functions. Interventions in Panama, Bosnia, Kosovo, and Libya are reviewed to learn the general context of each situation, stated US goals, US coercion strategy, means to employ coercion and the resulting end state. The cases show reaching a desired end state does not equal successful coercion.

Panama Invasion

As the Cold War was winding down, the US hoped for a more peaceful world that required less reliance on military force to execute foreign policy. This lofty belief was shaken from the start in Panama, a small country in Central America, where US interests in the shipping canal would compel action. This canal, built by the US in 1914, played a pivotal role for US strategic and commercial ventures for over six decades.[1] A 1978 treaty would pass control of the canal to Panama by 2000, although the US maintained security in the 5-mile canal zone until then. US security, for canal areas only, was provided by nearly 13,000 troops stationed at 142 US defense sites.[2]

Trouble began in Panama when, in June 1987, Panamanian Defense Force (PDF) leader Manuel Noriega was accused of murdering opposition leaders, electoral fraud, and

---

[1] Ronald H. Cole, *Operation Just Cause: The Planning and Execution of Joint Operations in Panama, February 1988 – January 1990* (Washington DC: Joint History Office, 1995), 5.

[2] Cole, 29; Jennifer M. Taw, *Operation Just Cause: Lessons for Operations Other Than War* (Santa Monica: Rand, 1996), 1.

involvement in the death of the previous dictator Omar Torrijos. Public protests followed these charges, which Noriega's PDF brutally put down.[3] The US Senate called for Noreiga to step down, resulting in a pro-Noriega mob attacking the US Embassy, which led President Reagan to halt all economic and military aid to Panama.[4] Additionally, on 4 February 1988, two US grand juries in Florida issued indictments against Noriega for racketeering and drug smuggling.[5] Panamanian President Delvalle fired Noriega, but the result was Delvalle's ouster.[6] With tensions rising between the self-appointed dictator and the US government, Noriega used anti-American rhetoric and harassment tactics against Americans in Panama to resist US coercion.

Attempts to coerce Panama and Noriega to operate within legal norms began with the diplomatic and economic sanctions previously mentioned. To counter this, Panama signed a trade agreement with the Soviet Union and stepped up harassment of US citizens in Panama.[7] Throughout 1988, the US State Department attempted to reassure Noriega the US would not intervene militarily and drop the drug indictments if he would step down.[8] Also during this period, NSA General Powell sided with Secretary of Defense Frank Carlucci and Joint Chiefs of Staff Chairman Admiral William Crowe against State Department advocacy of the use of force to restore Delvalle as President and overthrow

---

[3] Cole, 6.

[4] Edward M. Flanagan, Jr, *Battle for Panama: Inside Operation Just Cause* (Washington DC: Brassey's (US), Inc.,1993), 10.

[5] Ibid., 11.

[6] Taw, 4.

[7] Flanagan, 13-14.

[8] Taw, 5.

Noriega.[9] This position remained until the Reagan administration ended and the Bush administration began. In May 1989, Panama held presidential elections in which the opposition leader, Guillermo Endara, defeated Noriega's candidate.[10] Noriega declared the elections invalid and maintained control by sanctioning violence against the winners. As a result, President Bush deployed an additional 2,000 troops to Panama and increased training activities.[11] Secretary of Defense Richard Cheney stated the troops used for this deployment would not intervene in Panama to decide who governed, reassuring Noriega the troops were for security.[12] President Bush again urged Noriega to step down and move to a country that would not extradite him to the US.[13] Noriega responded by increasing rhetoric about the US creating a state of war with Panama and increasing harassment of US personnel.

President Bush, with congressional approval, had the Defense Department continue planning for activities in Panama with clear goals of protecting the canal and American citizens. An October 1989 failed coup attempt by Panamanian Major Giroldi further increased tensions.[14] The final straw came when Panamanian PDF personnel shot and killed US Marine Lieutenant Robert Paz, wounded another US officer, as well as detained and assaulted a US Navy officer and spouse that witnessed the event.[15] As a result of this event, along with the previous displayed patterns of brutality and corruption,

---

[9] Howard Means, *Colin Powell: Soldier/Statesman, Statesman/Soldier* (New York: Donald I. Fine, Inc., 1992), 248.

[10] Cole, 10.

[11] Flanagan, 16.

[12] Eytan Gilboa, "The Panama Invasion Revisited: Lessons for the Use of Force in the Post Cold War Era," *Political Science Quarterly* 110, no. 4 (Winter 1995): 549.

[13] Taw, 5.

[14] Cole, 14-15.

[15] Flanagan, 38-39.

President Bush decided force was required and ordered execution of Operation JUST CAUSE on December 17, 1989.[16] The operation consisted of approximately 27,000 US Air Force, Army, Navy, Marine Corps and special operations personnel in an integrated effort.[17] The operation began December 20 and combat operations ended by December 25, as PDF forces surrendered.[18] Noriega initially sought sanctuary in the Papal Nunciatura, but surrendered to US forces on 3 January 1990, was arrested and transported to the US by Drug Enforcement Agency officers. President Bush announced on January 3, 1990, that the operation's objectives were met and Operation JUST CAUSE ended 22 days later, on 11 January 1990, as efforts turned to stability and reconstruction operations.[19] By 31 January 1990, US military actions were complete.[20]

US Goals

Prior to Operation JUST CAUSE, President Bush described the political goals for Panama were to safeguard the lives of Americans, defend democracy in Panama, combat drug trafficking and protect the integrity of the Panama Canal Treaty.[21] Upon realization that diplomatic coercion was not going to achieve the goals due to the resistance of Noriega and his forces, Operation JUST CAUSE was given the mission to protect American lives, assist the democratically elected government, to seize and arrest an indicted drug trafficker, and to defend the integrity of US rights under the canal treaty.[22] General Thurman, Commander of United States Southern Command (USSOUTHCOM),

---

[16] Cole, 29-30.

[17] Taw, 12-13.

[18] Cole, 65.

[19] Ibid, 68-69.

[20] Taw, 28.

[21] Cole, 42.

[22] Taw, 9; Flanagan, 40.

translated the military objectives tasks as protect 30,000 US citizens, defend 142 key

facilities along the Panama canal, neutralize the PDF, neutralize the non-uniformed

Dignity Battalions (armed thugs working for Noriega), and capture Noriega himself.[23]

US Strategy

From 1987 until latter 1989, the US attempted to coerce Noriega's Panama

through sanctions, diplomatic pressure and shows of force by deploying troops to the

area. Noriega was not interested in accepting a deal that would end his power and he was

ready to continue operating in the manner unacceptable to the US. Noriega continued to

resist despite reassurance from the US State Department that American military force

would not be used to overthrow him, as well as President Bush's offer that if Noreiega

would step down he would not face extradition to the US for prosecution. The

Organization of American States (OAS) attempted to negotiate a settlement in the

summer and fall 1989, only to have Noriega's representatives tell them US aggression

should be dealt with rather than Noriega.[24] OAS representatives did criticize the US for

using sanctions, calling for a renewed settlement attempt; however, President Bush made

clear he would not abandon the effort to oust Noriega. If coercion was not successful,

military force would be used in a decisive, overwhelming fashion with clear, achievable

objectives.

Means

CJCS General Colin Powell directed USSOUTHCOM to plan a capability that

could deploy on short notice to address unforeseen contingencies in Panama, integrating

---

[23] Flanagan, 41.

[24] Ibid., 54.

special operations and conventional forces against unfriendly forces.[25] This changed from the previous plan in that forces would arrive rapidly rather than incrementally, in order to achieve surprise. The Weinberger and Powell doctrine previously described in Chapter 2 would generally be followed to achieve objectives in a reasonable time. The commander's guidance stated, "surprise the enemy by hitting first with overwhelming combat power under cover of night."[26] All elements of military force were planned for use, as needed to secure objectives, with no domains ruled out.

End State

The end state for Panama was simply to return the democratically elected government to power and in a position to rule. Additionally, Panama was to be a place safe for the US citizens living there and the canal was to operate safely, without fear of damage or closure by the government. Finally, Noriega was to be removed from power and arrested to stand trial for accused crimes.

Bosnian Civil War

With the demise of the Soviet Union came instability in many former member and partner nations. Yugoslavia, one of the former partner nations, leader of the Non-Aligned Nations, in southeast Europe, experienced this instability as several of its provinces began to secede from the Federation. In 1945, Marshal Tito (Josip Broz) the Yugoslavian communist dictator, redrew the internal boundaries of Yugoslavia to weaken Serbian influence.[27] Yugoslavia contained the provinces of Slovenia, Croatia, Bosnia-Herzegovina, Montenegro, Macedonia and Serbia, with Serbia containing the

---

[25] Ibid., 47.

[26] Ibid., 36.

[27] Alvin Z. Rubintstein, Albina Shayevich and Boris Zlotnikov, *The Clinton Foreign Policy Reader: Presidential Speeches with Commentary* (New York: M.E. Sharp, 2000), 166.

autonomous areas of Kosovo and Vojvodina. Tito held these disparate provinces together by imposing firm control and keeping the ethnic Serbian, Croatian, Slovene, and Bosniak Muslims separated to maintain Yugoslavian national identity. Following his death in 1980, the Presidency of Yugoslavia rotated among the leaders of the six provinces and two autonomous regions.[28] Ethnic groups began to push for autonomous nations and the Yugoslavian national identity waned. In 1985, the Serbian Academy of Sciences condemned Tito for anti-Serb policies and Serbian Party leader Slobodan Milosevic began to call for a greater Serbian state. The provinces of Slovenia, Croatia and Bosnia held referendums to secede from Yugoslavia and in June 1991 declared independence.[29] Despite some conflict between the Yugoslavian Army (JNA) and Croatian militia over Croatian secession, both Slovenia and Croatia became independent nations recognized by the European community. The Europeans did not recognize Bosnia and the JNA assisted Bosnian Serbs to fight secession.

Bosnia-Herzegovina contained a diverse population of about 40 percent Muslim, 17 percent Croatian and 30 percent Serbian.[30] These groups began to fight each other for control, with JNA supporting Bosnian Serbs, Croatia supporting the Bosnian Croats and the Bosnian Muslims (Bosniaks) fending for themselves. As the fighting grew, civilians were paying a heavy price, which led to the United Nations (UN) Security Council passing Resolution (UNSCR) 713 on September 25, 1991, calling for a cease-fire among

---

[28] Stathis N. Kalyvas and Nicholas Sambanis, "Bosnia's Civil War: Origins and Violence," In *Understanding Civil War,* vol 2 (Washington DC: Worldbank, 2005), 192.

[29] Ibid., 193.

[30] Ibid., 201.

all parties and imposed a weapons embargo on the Yugoslavian territories.[31] The

warring parties signed a cease-fire on November 23, 1991, Yugoslavia requested a

peacekeeping force to implement the agreement and the UN passed UNSCR 743 on

February 21, 1992, to deploy UN Protection Force (UNPROFOR) for an initial 12

months.[32]

US response to the brewing crisis in Bosnia was lukewarm, as President George

H.W. Bush was not ready to get the nation directly involved, preferring to let the

Europeans lead settlement of the matter. General Powell and the JCS resisted military

involvement in causes unless the reason for using force, clearly stated goals and its exit

strategy were determined.[33] Fighting continued and the UN passed UNSCR 752 on May

15, 1992, which called for Yugoslavia and Croatia to stay out of Bosnia and

implementation of the new cease-fire agreement signed April 12, 1992.[34] The UN passed

several more UNSCRs during 1992 implementing embargoes on weapons, increasing

diplomatic pressure and banning military flights in Bosnia. During the US presidential

campaign of 1992, the Democrat candidate, William Clinton, criticized President Bush

for failing to act to stop the violence.[35] After winning the election in 1992, President

Clinton would discover how complicated US involvement would be.

---

[31] United Nations Security Council, "Resolution 713, Cease Fire in Bosnia and Wepons Embargo in Yugoslavia," http://www.un.org/documents/res.htm, (accessed January 15, 2012).

[32] United Nations Security Council, "Resolution 743, Authorized a UN Protection Force," http://www.un.org/documents/res.htm, (accessed January 15, 2012).

[33] Dale R. Herspring, *The Pentagon and the Presidency: Civil-Military Relations from FDR to George W. Bush* (Lawrence: University Press of Kansas, 2005), 358.

[34] United Nations Security Council, "Resolution 752, Called for Yugoslavia and Croatia to Stay out of Bosnia," http://www.un.org/documents/res.htm, (accessed January 15, 2012).

[35] Derek Chollet and Bennett Freeman, *The Secret History of Dayton: US Diplomacy and the Bosnian Peace Process 1995*, (Washington DC: The National Security Archive, George Washington University, 2005), http://www.gwu.edu/~nsarchiv/NSAEBB/NSAEBB171/index.htm (accessed November 14, 2011), foreword.

Throughout 1993 and 1994 the UN passed UNSCRs to continue pressure. UNSCR 816 authorized member nations to take coordinated actions to enforce the no-fly ban and, with growing concern for Bosniaks, UNSCR 904 created five safe zone cities where UNPROFOR provided protection.[36] Using UNSCR 816, the North Atlantic Treaty Organization (NATO) began Operation DENY FLIGHT, the air defense campaign to enforce the no-fly zones beginning April 12, 1993, and continued this effort for nearly 1,000 days.[37] Bosnian Serbs stepped up the fighting despite UN and NATO efforts, so Bosniaks and Croats united to fight against them. Rising civilian casualties in Bosnia and refugees flowing to neighbor countries increased pressure on the President Clinton for US action.

Secretaries Christopher and Aspin were pushing for increased punitive airstrikes, but these ideas were not well received in Europe.[38] National Security Advisor (NSA) Lake pushed a plan to lift the weapons embargo to allow Bosniaks to get arms while increasing airstrikes on Bosnian Serbs; however, Europeans did not like this option as key allies felt a separate Muslim nation in Europe was unnatural.[39] The Clinton administration had consistently stated no US ground troops would be used; however, the UN continued to increase the size of the PROFOR with UNSCRs 904 and 914. Coalition indecision continued as the UN and NATO worked to resolve the fighting, fearing

[36] United Nations Security Council, "Resolution 816, No-fly Zone in Bosnia," "Resolution 904, Implemented Muslim Safe Zones," http://www.un.org/documents/res.htm, (accessed January 15, 2012).

[37] Air Force Historical Studies Office, *Operation DENY FLIGHT Fact Sheet*, http://www.afhso.af.mil/topics/factsheet/factsheet.asp?id=15872. Accessed 5 Feb 2012

[38] Nigel Hamilton, *Bill Clinton: Mastering the Presidency* (New York: Persius Books Group, 2007), 126-127.

[39] Taylor Branch, *The Clinton Tapes: Wrestling History with the President* (New York: Simon and Schuster, 2009), 9.

escalation to neighboring countries. Ethnic cleansing of Bosniaks by Bosnian Serbs surfaced in latter 1994, and UNSCR 941 demanded it stop.[40] Bosnian Serbs would not stop, but rather escalated the attacks.

UNPROFOR personnel had consistently used a policy of monitoring, expecting the Bosnians to honor signed cease-fire agreements. In May 1995, Bosnian Serbs not only attacked the UNPROFOR safe areas, but also took UNPROFOR personnel as hostages to deter NATO airstrikes.[41] NATO responded to this tactic by authorizing a Rapid Reaction Force that could go in to evacuate UNPROFOR, with President Clinton stating the US would support a temporary force for withdrawal purpose.[42] On July 6, 1995, the Bosnian Serbs attacked Srebrinca, murdering and driving out thousands of Bosniaks.[43] This was the final straw to make President Clinton decide on a strategy to force the warring factions to the negotiating table. "Europeans could not handle the worsening crisis without provoking war; ergo the US would have to take charge, unilaterally if necessary, and force the Serbs to the negotiating table by force—air force."[44] The US tried again to coerce Bosnian Serbs to withdraw forces and negotiate, but their intransigence led NATO to execute Operation DELIBERATE FORCE, the airstrikes on Serb positions in Bosnia from August 30 to September 14, 1995, when the Serbs agreed and withdrew. A negotiated peace settlement occurred in Dayton, Ohio, led by the US with Bosnia, Croatia and Serb leaders signing an agreement that used NATO

---

[40] United Nations Security Council, "Resolution 941, Demanded Ethnic Cleansing Cease," http://www.un.org/documents/res.htm, (accessed January 15, 2012).

[41] Chollet and Freeman, 2.

[42] Ibid., 4.

[43] Ibid., 16.

[44] Hamilton, 493.

and UN forces to administer the country and peace.[45] The US committed to sending one-third of the 36,000 NATO force to the effort with President Clinton saying, "I am satisfied the NATO implementation plan is clear, limited, achievable and the risks to troops are minimized."[46] US troops completed their contribution to the UN mission in Bosnia in 2004, however UN peacekeepers remain in Bosnia.

US Goals

Initially, the goal was to let Europe resolve the matter with US providing diplomatic support through United Nations Security Council (UNSC) efforts. As Clinton entered the Presidency, the administration wanted a separate Bosnia with ten separate cantons.[47] Then the goal became containing the violence to Bosnia-Herzegovina and finally turned to stopping the humanitarian crises. In a July 1994 speech, President Clinton expressed four US goals in Yugoslavia as preventing spread of fighting; stemming the flow of refugees; halting the slaughter of innocents; and helping confirm NATO's role in post-Cold War Europe.[48]

US Strategy

From 1991 until mid 1993, the US used diplomacy to coerce the warring factions in Bosnia to negotiate peace. With the UNSC setting the stage, weapons embargoes and no-fly zones were added to step up pressure, unfortunately little consequence occurred for violators. The US wanted to increase the threat of force, but stopped short with air power, insisting the problem was not a significant enough interest to employ ground

---

[45] Ibid., 518.

[46] Ibid., 549.

[47] Rubintstein, Shayevich, and Zlotnikov, 167.

[48] Ibid., 32.

troops. By summer 1995, Secretary of Defense Perry and CJCS General Shalikashvili said the only way to stop Bosnian Serbs was to threaten overwhelming military force.[49] When violence reached unacceptable limits with the Serbs murdering thousands of Bosniaks under view of UNPROFOR, the US increased air strikes to unacceptable limits to the Serbs and resulted in a negotiated settlement.

Means

The US employed diplomacy to support UN-mandated sanctions. When these sanctions did not achieve the desired effects due to lack of enforcement, the US supported no-fly zones over Bosnia with US military aircraft. No ground troops was the consistent theme of the Administration; however, ground troops were presented as an option to help withdraw UNPROFOR if needed, but not for coercive purposes. When Sebian atrocities reached unacceptable proportions, US air power was applied in concert with Croat and Bosniak ground elements to drive the Serbians to accept a negotiated settlement. Finally, thousands of US ground troops were employed to enforce the final peace agreement negotiated in Dayton, Ohio, and later signed in Paris.

End State

The US first wanted to stop violence, with warring factions working to settle disputes peacefully. The US planned to recognize a separate Bosnia-Herzegovina, which the UN recognized and admitted to the UN with UNSCR 755 in May 1992. Then a proposed settlement brokered by Cyrus Vance would settle the dispute with a federated Bosnia with 10 cantons, though this was voted down by referendum.[50] Finally, the

---

[49] Chollet and Freeman, 18.

[50] Hamilton, 127.

Dayton Accords achieved a Bosnia-Herzegovina, with two semi-autonomous entities.[51]

The country was split 51 percent to Federation Bosnia-Herzegovina (Muslims and

Croats) while 49 percent went to Republika Srpska (Bosnian Serbs), each with a

parliament. The nation consists of ten cantons for policing and administration, and each

of three main factions can block a federal decision if it feels the effort against their vital

interest. UN forces remain in Bosnia monitoring progress and implementing

governmental controls in 2012.

Kosovo Ethnic Cleansing

As with Bosnia-Herzegovina, ethnic strife in the former Yugoslavian areas spilled

into Kosovo. Kosovo had been recognized as an autonomous region, with its own

assembly to govern until 1990, when Serbian President Slobodan Milosevic revoked the

autonomy and ruled the area from Belgrade.[52] Kosovo was an area mainly populated by

Muslims, but was very important to Serbian history and an area Milosevic used to rally

Serbian nationalism. Kosovars responded to the takeover by declaring Kosovo a

republic, setting the stage for increased tensions in the region.[53]

During the 1990s, Kosovars continued to live under Serbian rule as an underclass,

with abuses continuing to rise.[54] Brutal aggression by Serbian police and military

brought out resistance. The Kosovo Liberation Army (KLA), founded by Kosovar

Hashim Thaci, began mounting attacks against Serbian police and attacking Serbian areas

---

[51] Congressional Research Service, *Bosnia: Current Issues and US Policy, A Study Prepared for Members and Comittees of Congress by the Congressional Research Service, June 20, 2011* (Washington DC: Government Printing Office, 2011), 2.

[52] Kalyvas and Sambanis, 192.

[53] Ibid., 192.

[54] Richard Sale, *Clinton's Secret Wars The Evolution of a Commander in Chief* (New York: St Martin's Press, 2009), 318-319.

with terrorist tactics to resist further oppression.[55] The Serbs responded by surrounding

entire towns, shelling them with artillery and tanks, capturing women and boys, and

executing the men while burning the buildings.[56] The international community was

about to act in the internal matters of a sovereign nation.

With hundreds of thousands of Kosovar civilians displaced, the contact group of

Russia, US, France, Germany, Great Britain and Italy met and decided the violence

needed to end and dialogue begin between warring parties to solve the crisis.[57] President

Clinton made clear the US would not wait while the UN or NATO nibbled at the edges

for two and a half years as had been done in Bosnia.[58] The UN passed UNSCR 1160 in

March 1998 imposing an arms embargo on Yugoslavia and called on the parties to

negotiate.[59] The fighting continued and NATO conducted an airpower show of force,

Operation DETERMINED FALCON, to convince Serbia the fighting must stop.[60] These

pressures did not stop the Serbians, resulting in UNSCRs 1199 and 1203, which

demanded a ceasefire and outside observers to verify compliance.[61] Initially Milosevic

balked, but the threat of NATO airstrikes brought about his agreement. Serbia was to

reduce the Yugoslav military and police forces in Kosovo, both parties were to cease

fighting, and displaced people were to be allowed to return home. Unfortunately,

---

[55] Ibid., 319.

[56] Ibid., 320.

[57] Congressional Research Service, *Kosovo: Review and Analysis of Policy Objectives, 1998-Jun 1999: A Study Prepared for Members and Commitees of Congress by the Congressional Research Service, July 1999* (Washington DC: Government Printing Office, 1999), 3.

[58] Sale, 322.

[59] Congressional Research Service, *Kosovo: Review and Analysis,* 4.

[60] Dag Henricksen, "Inflexible Response: Diplomacy, Airpower and the Kosovo Crisis, 1998-1999," *The Journal of Strategic Studies* 31, no. 6 (December 2008): 836.

[61] United Nations Security Council, "Resolution 1199, Kosovo Cease Fire," "Resolution 1203, Observers in Kosovo," http://www.un.org/documents/res.htm, (accessed January 15, 2012).

violations on each side led to additional atrocities resulting in renewed attempts by the international community to resolve the crisis.

Peace talks took place February 1999 in Rambouillet to achieve autonomy for Kosovo secured by an international security force.[62] The Kosovars signed the agreement but Serbia refused, because Milosevic knew if he lost Kosovo his political career would be finished at home.[63] Serbia mounted an offensive, Operation Horseshoe, meant to seize Kosovo and permanently displace 800,000 Kosovars.[64] Outraged, the US led NATO to begin Operation ALLIED FORCE, the air operation to force Milosevic to accept the Ramboullet agreement. Disagreements within NATO as to what, where and how things should be bombed occurred; however, the operations continued for 78 days until Milosevic agreed to terms.[65] According to General Wesley Clark, Supreme Allied Commander in Europe for NATO, the final factors for Milosevic must have been lack of outside assistance, no support from Russia and increasingly hostile neighbors with declining support at home.[66] Serbians withdrew from Kosovo, and it became an autonomous area with a NATO-led peacekeeping force of 50,000 maintaining order. Border disputes between the Kosovars and Serbians continue to occur and US troops are expected to remain through at least 2013.[67]

---

[62] Congressional Research Service, *Kosovo: Review and Analysis*, 5.

[63] Sale, 349.

[64] Ibid., 351.

[65] Ibid., 381.

[66] Wesley K. Clark, *Waging Modern War: Bosnia, Kosovo, and the Future of Combat* (New York: Public Affairs, 2001), 406.

[67] Beta, "US Troops til' at Least Jun 2013," B92, http://www.b92.net/eng/news/politics-article.php?yyyy=2012&mm=01&dd=04&nav_id=78118.

US Goals

As stated in President Clinton's 13 December 1998 White House address, the goals in Kosovo were to protect thousands of innocent people from the mounting Serbian military offensive, prevent a wider war, act to stand united with our allies, and uphold our values, protect our interests, and advance the cause for peace.[68] Further stated objectives for Operation ALLIED FORCE were demonstrate the seriousness of NATO's purpose, deter a bloodier offensive by Yugoslavia, and limit Milosevic's ability to make war in Kosovo.[69]

US Strategy

The US diplomatic effort worked to resolve the conflict through international pressure and UN authorized sanctions. To improve sanction effectiveness, NATO shows of force were used to convince Serbians of NATO credibility. Blatant disregard for the UN mandates resulted in the US leading NATO in punitive airstrikes to bring Milosevic to accept an international agreed settlement, even without UN force authorization. The US did provide ground troops to implement the signed peace agreement and remains in Kosovo working resolution of the original governance problem.

Means

The US used diplomacy and sanctions tied to UN-mandates under UNSCRs. The experience of Bosnia had taught the Clinton Administration further means might be necessary when dealing with Milosevic, so airstrikes occurred without direct UN authorization. Additionally, despite the President declaring no troops in Kosovo to fight

---

[68] Rubintstein, Shayevich, and Zlotnikov, 190.

[69] Congressional Research Service, *Kosovo: Review and Analysis*, 6.

a war, US troops were at the border ready to move in at the end of the 11-week bombing campaign, with relief planning underway and funding appropriated by Congress.[70]

End State

The conflict in Kosovo ended with Serbian withdrawal from Kosovo and the KLA disarmed. NATO led a Kosovo Force (KFOR) to repopulate refugees and monitor peace to prevent recurring violence. Kosovo has established a government and operates autonomously with KFOR and US troops expected to remain through 2013.[71]

Libyan Civil War

In February 2011, opposition groups within Libya rose up against the dictator Muammar al Qadhafi, who had led Libya since a 1969 revolution.[72] Groups in several cities began to demonstrate against the government and the police and security forces attempted to quell their protests violently. The protestors fought back, taking control of some Libyan cities. Qadhafi responded by threatening to kill them and show no mercy.[73]

The international community responded with UNSCR 1970 on February 26, 2011, to freeze assets and impose travel bans and economic sanctions.[74] Qadhafi ignored the restrictions and used his security and military forces to pound rebel positions, killing civilians in the cities he believed stood against his authority. Killing civilians increased

---

[70] Thomas W. Lippman, *Madeline Albright and the New American Diplomacy* (Boulder: Westview Press, 2002), 101.

[71] Beta, "US Troops til' at Least Jun 2013," B92, http://www.b92.net/eng/news/politics-article.php?yyyy=2012&mm=01&dd=04&nav_id=78118.

[72] Congressional Research Service, *Libya: Unrest and U.S Policy; A Study Prepared for Members and Committees of Congress, by the Congressional Research Service, March 2011* (Washington DC: Government Printing Office, 2011), 1.

[73] The White House, "We Have Already Saved Lives," The Press Office, http://www.whitehouse.gov/blog/2011/03/22/president-libya-we-have-already-saved-lives (accessed August 19, 2011).

[74] United Nations Security Council, "Resolution 1170, Sanctions on Libya," UNSC, http://www.un.org/documents/res.htm, (accessed January 15, 2012).

calls for military intervention by Western powers, with Secretary of State Clinton insisting no options were off the table while Secretary of Defense Gates warned military intervention was no small matter and Libya was not a vital interest of the US.[75] A month passed with increased rhetoric from politicians while the conflict continued.

UNSCR 1973 passed on 18 March, authorizing participating nations to take action to enforce a no-fly zone and embargo in Libya.[76] President Obama announced US forces would enforce the no-fly zone to protect Libyan civilians, stabilize the region and uphold our democratic values.[77] The attempt to coerce Qadhafi through diplomacy and sanctions had failed, requiring allies to increase pressure with force.

UN sanctions never called for Qadhafi to step down; however, US and other Western leaders did. The US began Operation ODYSSEY DAWN on March 19, 2011, using air strikes to protect civilians, ostensibly aiding the rebel forces at the same time. By the end of March, NATO officially took lead for the military effort; however, a large number of assets were contributed by the US Rebel forces succeeded in taking over the country, making their declaration of liberation and getting UN recognition on October 23, 2011. NATO forces terminated the no-fly zone October 31, 2011, with the UN agreeing

[75] Voice of America, *Clinton: Libyan Rebels Oppose Outside Intervention*, State Department, http://www.voanews.com/english/news/Clinton-Says-All-Options-Open-on-Libya-117155238.html ; Star Advertiser, *Gates Downplays Possible Military Intervention in Libya*, Associated Press, http://www.staradvertiser.com/news/breaking/117211733.html?id=117211733 (accessed February 11, 2012).

[76] United Nations Security Council, "Resolution 1973, Authorized Force to Enforce a No-fly Zone," http://www.un.org/documents/res.htm, (accessed January 15, 2012).

[77] The White House, *Our Goal is Focused, Our Cause Just and Our Coalition is Strong*, The Press Office, http://www.whitehouse.gov/blog/2011/03/18/president-libya-our-goal-focused-our-cause-just-and-our-coalition-strong (accessed August 19, 2011).

to keep some assistance forces in Libya through March 16, 2012 to assist the Transitional Government in Libya.[78]

US Goals

President Obama's stated US goals were to protect civilians, stabilize the region and uphold democratic values. The mission later expanded to assist the departure of Muammar Qadhafi and support selection of a new government by the Libyan people.

US Strategy

The US strategy leveraged UN and NATO organizations to gain consensus on action required to resolve the crisis in Libya. The US then used UN authorization to join NATO allies to force resolution, initially with coercive diplomacy moving to forced compliance. US and UN goals differed as the UN never called for Qadhafi's ouster, making successful coercion more difficult.

Means

Diplomacy, sanctions and freezing assets combined to pressure compliance from the Libyan regime. When this did not achieve success, increased pressure through military force, air only, struck the regime and aided rebel forces to compel compliance.

End State

The US wanted Libya free from the dictator Qadhafi, with process in place to install a freely elected democratic government that protects its citizens. As previously mentioned, the UN never called for the removal of Qadafhi.

---

[78] United Nations Security Council, "Resolution 2016, Recognized Transitional Government," http://www.un.org/documents/res.htm, (accessed January 15, 2012).

With the described coercion cases presented, the following chapter will present analysis of each to determine what lessons can be drawn to make future coercion attempts more successful.

CHAPTER 4: ANALYSIS AND RECOMMENDATIONS

Coercion uses the threat or use of an instrument (e.g. airstrike) applied to a mechanism (e.g. power base erosion) to achieve a desired outcome (e.g. regime change).[1] Successfully achieving objectives may not mean successful coercion; however, as military force may be required to force compliance rather than coerce the adversary decision. The coercion attempts presented in Chapter 3 will be analyzed to determine coercion success in terms of a consistent and clear message, the credible expectation of the use of threatened military force and a military threat capable of imposing the coercer's demands. This analysis will offer some implications to help make threat of military force more consistent, credible and appear more capable in future operations and may lead to coercion that is more successful.

Panama Invasion

As former Secretary of Defense Weinberger points out, the United States (US) operation in Panama was a complete success.[2] The end state desired by the US was achieved upon completion of the mission; however, coercion was not successful as military force was used to force the desired outcome leaving no decision for Noriega. The US used diplomacy and troop presence, added sanctions, then added shows of force with more troops and exercises to deny Noriega success, only to resort to employment of military force for regime change. Noriega attempted to counter with outside agreements and getting Organization of American States (OAS) support. Though a successful

---

[1] Daniel Byman and Matthew Waxman, *The Dynamics of Coercion: American Foreign Policy and the Limits of Military Might*, (New York: Cambridge University Press, 2002), 27.

[2] Caspar Weinberger, *Fighting for Peace: Seven Critical Years in the Pentagon* (New York: Warner Books, 1990), 12.

military operation that achieved the desired end state, the effort to coerce Noriega was unsuccessful due to inconsistent demands and lack of credibility regarding the threatened use of force.

Consistent and Clear Message

US officials undermined the effort to coerce Noriega by sending mixed and confused signals.[3] The US had supported Noriega and used him in anti-communist efforts in the early-to-mid 1980s, ignoring the problems he caused in Panama as an internal matter.[4] As problems grew to crisis level in 1987, President Reagan attempted to coerce Noriega by cutting military and economic aid to convince him to behave in a manner consistent with international law while the US Senate called for Noriega to step down. In December 1987, Assistant Secretary of Defense for International Affairs, Richard Armitage, met with Noriega to reinforce this message, but was instead seen with Noriega laughing and drinking scotch.[5] Coercion was further diluted by US State Department reassurance to Noriega that the US would not use its military to intervene in Panamanian governance, while Treasury Secretary James Baker also stated publicly that the things the US could do with Panama involved military action and which the US would not do.[6] Noriega's behavior did not change, but President Reagan took no more action.[7]

---

[3] Eytan Gilboa, "The Panama Invasion Revisited: Lessons for the Use of Force in the Post Cold War Era," *Political Science Quarterly* 110, no. 4 (Winter 1995): 540.

[4] Ibid., 539.

[5] Ibid., 544.

[6] Ibid., 545.

[7] Dale R. Herspring, *The Pentagon and the Presidency: Civil-Military Relations from FDR to George W. Bush* (Lawrence: University Press of Kansas, 2005), 303.

In 1989, President Bush increased pressure to coerce Noriega to step down with shows of military force, continued sanctions and freezing of Panamanian assets in the US Unfortunately, during this same timeframe Secretary of Defense Richard Cheney stated the increased troops would not intervene in Panama to determine who governed, while the Treasury Department granted so many exemptions to the economic sanctions they simply punished the Panamanian people and did little to influence Noriega.[8] These inconsistent messages undermined coercion and removed credibility from the threatened use of military force.

Credible Expectation of the Use of Military Force

As mentioned, Noreiga had worked with many senior US government officials during the 1980s and felt the threat of military force against him was not credible. This lack of credibility was reinforced with statements from the State, Defense and Treasury Departments to reassure Noriega the US would not intervene to remove him. Further, when Panamanian Defense Force Major Moises Giroldi attempted a coup in October, 1989, and requested US assistance, the US did not act.[9] Additionally, Noriega had some success in getting the OAS to criticize US sanctions and call for renewed diplomatic efforts, likely leading Noriega to believe he had outside support against US military intervention. Once the credibility for the threat of military force was lost and officials realized sanctions and diplomacy failed, the decision came to employ force.

---

[8] Gilboa, 547, 549.

[9] Ronald H. Cole, *Operation Just Cause: The Planning and Execution of Joint Operations in Panama, February 1988 – January 1990* (Washington DC: Joint History Office, 1995), 15.

A Capable Military Threat

The US employed a combined arms force of 27,000 personnel in overwhelming fashion to defeat Panamanian forces, capture Noreiga and extradite him to the US for prosecution. This force was more than capable to force Noriegan compliance, however, the lack of credibility made Noriega believe the US would not employ it. Vice President Quayle described the operation as a JUST CAUSE, precisely defined objectives, with no skimping on the military might the job required.[10] Unfortunately, no matter how capable a military force, it cannot coerce if the adversary does not think the force will be used.

Bosnian Civil War

The effort to coerce Bosnian warring parties began poorly as the international community initially failed to recognize Bosnian independence, the US refused to be involved and later refused ground troops. The United Nations (UN) applied and eased sanctions to weaken the parties and force a negotiated settlement, but failed to enforce the sanctions. Failure to respond to mandate violations and unclear commitment from allies further reduced credibility of the coercive effort. The Bosnian Serbs counter-coerced by taking hostages and attacking Muslim safe areas, forcing the US to call for increased action. Civilian atrocities compelled the coalition to increase pressure and the UN authorized Operation DELIBERATE FORCE, the North Atlantic Treaty Organization (NATO)-led airstrikes. The airstrikes, combined with threat of Croatian ground forces coerced the Serbs to accept UN mandates and a negotiated peace settlement.[11] While

---

[10] Dan Quayle, *Standing Firm: A Vice Presidential Memoir*, (New York: Harper-Collins Publishers, 1994) 149.

[11] Byman and Waxman, 120-121.

some grade this coercion as a partial success, inconsistent messages, lack of a credible

threat of force and reduced military capability delayed achieving the desired ending.[12]

Consistent and Clear Message

The European community did not recognize Bosnian independence when declared

in 1991, as they had done for Croatia and Slovenia. This lack of support led Yugoslavia

to support Bosnian Serbs in effort to stop the cessation through military force. President

Bush viewed the war as a European problem to solve and did not inject US involvement.

The UN passed numerous Security Council Resolutions (UNSCR) to impose a weapons

embargo, a no-fly zone, organize cease-fires, and recognize Bosnia as a nation, but took

little effort to punish or stop violators of the mandates as many viewed a European

Muslim country unnatural.

President Clinton called for a separate Bosnia with 10 cantons, as the preeminent

US interest was to keep the war from spreading.[13] This idea was not supported as UN

Secretary General Boutros-Ghali insisted Muslim enclaves in the Balkans were doomed

as illegitimate.[14] A UN Protection Force (UNPROFOR) was sent to Bosnia to enforce

peace, but they had strict orders not to resist attack and were often more hindrance than

help. From 1992 until the fall of 1995, repeated messages from the UN, US and other

nations calling for Bosnian Serbs to stop fighting and negotiate a settlement were

ignored, while repeated threats of force to stop the Bosnian Serbs were never effectively

---

[12] Michael I. Handel, Masters of War: Classical Strategic Thought, Third Edition (Portland: Frank Cass Publishers, 2001), 326; Kelly M. Greenhill, Weapons of Mass Migration: Forced Displacement, Coercion and Foreign Policy (Ithaca: Cornell University Press, 2010), 33.

[13] Taylor Branch, *The Clinton Tapes: Wrestling History with the President* (New York: Simon and Schuster, 2009), 217.

[14] Ibid., 55.

acted upon. These mixed messages caused the Serbs to doubt the credibility of threatened force.

Credible Expectation of the Use of Military Force

In 1992, the UN established UNPROFOR in Bosnia to observe the warring parties of the cease-fire agreement. Unfortunately, the factions continued to fight while UNPROFOR troops merely watched. Next, the UN authorized nations to enforce previously mandated sanctions and a no-fly zone, resulting in the NATO led Operation DENY FLIGHT. Rather than successfully enforce mandates, this effort was merely a bluff stitched over objections from countries with troops deployed as part of UNPROFOR and afraid of Serb retaliation.[15] Further, President Clinton repeatedly stated no US ground troops would be deployed to Bosnia, which left air power the only credible threat. US Air Force Chief of Staff, General McPeak, told the Senate, "not to expect too much from air power in the Balkans as mountainous terrain, foliage and bad weather would prevent the kind of success seen in the Gulf War."[16] Continued fighting, led by the Bosnian Serbs, went undeterred as the attempt to use American bombs in Operation DENY FLIGHT proved a complete failure due to UN and NATO hesitation.[17] The situation remained unchanged until the Serbs took UNPROFOR troops hostage and attacked Muslim civilians in Srebrinca. The NATO-led Operation DELIBERATE FORCE applied enough air power, combined with the ground offensive by Bosnian Croat and Muslim ground forces, caused the Serbs to accept a negotiated peace. Though ultimately successful in achieving a desired end, the threat of force was not credible for

---

[15] Ibid., 120.

[16] Paul C. Forage, "Bombs for Peace: A Comparative Study of the Use of Air Power in the Balkans," *Armed Forces and Society* 28, No. 2 (Winter 2002): 216.

[17] Nigel Hamilton, *Bill Clinton: Mastering the Presidency* (New York: Persius Books Group, 2007), 480.

nearly four years due to failure to back up stated threats and restrictions that reduced capability of the force used.

A Capable Military Threat

A capable military threat implies the threatened force will have the capability to force someone to do something they do not want to do. As discussed previously, the UNPROFOR was not effective due to orders not to intervene, but merely observe actions. Serbian forces quickly learned this force would not prevent their actions and ignored the UNPROFOR presence. Subsequent UN-authorized force through NATO led-Operation DENY FLIGHT was also ineffective due to a hesitance to employ force along with the lack of ground force support. Air power, while it has the advantage of limiting casualty exposure and having the ability to withdraw quickly, also has the disadvantage of not being on the ground to actually force uncooperative actors.[18] US administration officials were split on involvement in Bosnia, with some arguing for intervention while others opposed. According to General Sullivan, "Europeans were looking for leadership from the US with troops on the ground, but it was not forthcoming, only air."[19] Not until the US-led effort to combine effective NATO airstrikes in Operation DELIBERATE FORCE, combined with Croat and Muslim ground force maneuver, did the Serbians realize the military threat was truly capable of defeating them and coerce their agreement

---

[18] Robert C. Owen, "An American View of Peace Support Operations: A Perspective on Air Power," In *From Maneuver Warfare to Kosovo?* (Norway: The Royal Norwegian Air Force Academy, 2006), 124.

[19] Hamilton, 131.

71

to a negotiated settlement.[20] "Three and a half years of fiddling while Sarajevo burned were over."[21]

Kosovo Ethnic Cleansing

The US took a more active role in Kosovo, learning from the Bosnian effort. Diplomatic calls to end violence were followed with sanctions, shows of force and later airstrikes that weakened, punished and denied Serbian gains to compel compliance. The effort to coerce Serbia was successful in achieving escalation dominance to change behavior, but only earns a partially successful rating, as all objectives were not achieved.[22] Coercion was successful in achieving the stated goals of ending a humanitarian crisis, producing a military situation conducive to peace, and demonstrating NATO unity and resolve; but was unsuccessful in achieving a durable political settlement that would resolve the ultimate cause of the conflict.[23] As a result of not achieving a durable political settlement, US and NATO troops remain in Kosovo for continued containment. Though the coercion was not completely successful in achieving all goals, the effort was a success in having a consistent and clear demand to the adversary. The credibility of the military force threat and capability of the force used were degraded, however, due to limitations that should not have been announced to Serbia.

Consistent and Clear Message

The international community did not support the Kosovo population in their claim to independence from Serbia, indicating to the Serbians the matter could be resolved

---

[20] Forage, 222-223.

[21] Hamilton, 514.

[22] Handel, 326.

[23] Congressional Research Service, *Kosovo: Review and Analysis of Policy Objectives, 1998-Jun 1999: prepared for members and commitees of Congress by the Congressional Research Service, July 1999* (Washington DC: Government Printing Office, 1999), 8-12.

internally.[24] Following the Serbian atrocities against Kosovar civilians, the US message

remained constant in demanding an end to violence and that the conflict be resolved

through negotiation. UNSCRs established the sanctions, embargoes and negotiation

demands, however, the Serbians and Kosovars both violated the mandates. NATO

organized the Rambouillet Peace talks in February 1999 to again try to end the violence

and achieve autonomy for Kosovo, but the Serbians rejected the offer and increased

violent attacks despite NATO-threatened airstrikes for non-compliance. The US and

NATO responded to Serbian aggression with Operation ALLIED FORCE, which

compelled Milosevic to agree to NATO terms. A consistent and clear message with

increased pressure compelled the adversary to agree to coercive demands, though actions

did occur to reduce credibility of the use of military force.

Credible Expectation of the Use of Military Force

As discussed earlier, Serbian leader Milosevic had dealt with NATO and US

military threats in Bosnia, so his experience likely influenced his behavior in Kosovo.

The declaration by President Clinton that US ground troops would not fight a war in

Kosovo arguably solidified Milosevic's idea he could resist US and NATO threats.

Additionally, several US administration officials made statements indicating Kosovo

would be a short war, furthering the belief that US commitment to support the Kosovars

was not strong.[25] NATO did use a show of force with airpower in Operation

DETERMINED FALCON, however, with no UN authorization to use force Milosevic

was not likely to take the threat seriously. Rather than obtaining a UNSCR to authorize

---

[24] Ibid., 2.

[25] Richard Sale, *Clinton's Secret Wars The Evolution of a Commander in Chief* (New York: St Martin's Press, 2009), 349; Secretary Albright also stated in a PBS interview 24 Mar 1999 with Jim Lehrer, "I don't see this as a long term operation."

force, President Clinton said UNSCR 1199 was enough language to legally compel Milosevic's compliance with UN demands, by force if necessary.[26] The military threat was implemented despite lacking credibility, though military capability was also reduced.

A Capable Military Threat

President Clinton made clear, "I do not intend to put our troops in Kosovo to fight a war," when he addressed the nation on December 13, 1998.[27] Political leaders had taken many military options off the table and decided to use air power to alter Serbian behavior.[28] The use of airpower was successful in coercing Milosevic, however, limits on the type of force applied delayed the result. Airstrikes were less effective due to no available ground force to help identify targets or fix enemy ground forces to enable aircraft to strike them.[29] Additionally, enemy anti-aircraft weapons and small arms, unhindered by a friendly ground force, created a hazard that required NATO aircraft to fly higher altitudes where they were less effective.[30] Ultimately, reducing the effectiveness of the military threat by reducing capbility increased the time for success and encouraged the adversary to resist coercion.

Libyan Civil War

The international community, outraged by the Libyan leader Qadhafi's ordered killing of civilians, attempted to coerce Qadhafi to stop. The US called for restraint from Qadhafi, but was hesitant to become actively involved beyond diplomacy. UN sanctions

---

[26] Congressional Research Service, *Kosovo: Review and Analysis,* 4.

[27] Alvin Z. Rubintstein, Albina Shayevich and Boris Zlotnikov, *The Clinton Foreign Policy Reader: Presidential Speeches with Commentary* (New York: M.E. Sharp, 2000), 192.

[28] Michael C. Short, "An Airman's Lessons from Kosovo," In *From Maneuver Warfare to Kosovo?* (Norway: The Royal Norwegian Air Force Academy, 2006), 259.

[29] Ibid., 263.

[30] Ibid., 263.

and embargoes were imposed to weaken Libya, but Qadhafi's quickly increasing attacks on civilians forced UN escalation. The UN authorized force to protect civilians and enforce sanctions, so Libyan Foreign Minister Moussa Koussa announced Libya would halt military actions as directed by the UNSCR.[31] President Obama issued the ultimatum to Qadhafi, honor the UN mandates and allow humanitarian aid to Libyan people or face consequences imposed through military action.[32] Qadhafi resisted coercion, continued attacks on civilians and refused to change his behavior or relinquish his national power. The message was clear, though ignored by Qadhafi, and airstrikes began March 19, 2011.

Consistent and Clear Message

The US message was initially clear, insisting Qadhafi stop harming civilians and accept a negotiated settlement with his people. The UN passed a resolution to impose sanctions and demand a cease-fire. When that was ignored by Qadhafi, the US increased the demand by insisting that Qadhafi must relinquish power, a demand never stated by the UN. This demand was partially weakened, however, when US Secretary of Defense Robert Gates urged caution, indicating there was no unanimity in NATO and urging the US not get into another large land war.[33] The UN passed a resolution authorizing force to impose a no-fly zone and protect civilians, to which NATO, led by the US, began an air campaign to assist rebel forces oust Qadhafi. Unfortunately, statements and actions had undermined the credibility of the threat of that force.

---

[31] Tyler Durden, "Libyan Foreign Minister Announces Immediate Cease-fire," *Reuters*, March 18, 2011.

[32] Daniel Dombey and Richard McGregor, "Obama Delivers Qadhafi Ultimatum," *The Financial Times*, March 18, 2011,

[33] David Sanger and Thom Shanker, "Gates Warns of Risks of a No-Fly Zone," *The New York Times*, March 2, 2011.

Credible Expectation of the Use of Military Force

Qadhafi likely doubted the credibility of the threat of force coming from the U.S and some allies due to differences in international opinion and statements from senior US officials regarding use of force and duration of US involvement. When the UN passed the resolution authorizing military force, Russia, China, India, Germany and Brazil all abstained and stated military action was not an option at this time.[34] When President Obama addressed the American public from the White House on March 18, 2011, he stated, "the United States is not going to deploy ground troops to Libya," clearly indicating an air only threat.[35] Additionally, President Obama stated the US would be involved for days, not months, clearly giving the impression to Qadhafi that the US demand could be waited out.[36] Qadhafi had been in power over 40 years and had faced conflict with Western powers previously and survived, giving him further reason to believe the threat lacked credibility even if capable of decapitating his regime.

A Capable Military Threat

At the outset, President Obama stated there would be no ground troops, reducing capability of the force. However, unlike Kosovo, NATO was able to coordinate with ground forces to aid aerial attacks. Additionally, the terrain and weather conditions favored airstrikes, allowing the NATO air campaign to be effective. The effort lasted from March until October, longer than originally predicted by President Obama, but was successful in enabling the ouster of Qadhafi while preventing major attacks on civilians.

---

[34] Sara A. Carter, "UN Authorizes No-Fly Zone Over Libya," *The Examiner*, March 17, 2011.

[35] The White House, *Our Goal is Focused, Our Cause Just and Our Coalition is Strong*, The Press Office, http://www.whitehouse.gov/blog/2011/03/18/president-libya-our-goal-focused-our-cause-just-and-our-coalition-strong (accessed August 19, 2011).

[36] Ibid.

Implications for Future Coercion

The cited cases show that consistent objectives, backed by credible and capable coercive instruments combine to provide the best chance of successful coercion. Coercive instruments have to be aimed at specific pressure points in order to influence the areas the adversary needs the most, providing the most pressure to coerce decision making. Ultimately, to have the best chance of successful coercion, US leaders must develop a sound strategy for coercion at the outset and be committed to increasing pressure over time. Unfortunately, sometimes policy makers enter conflicts with no coercive strategy at all.[37] Lack of strategy leads to hesitation and inconsistent demands, leading adversaries to doubt credibility and, ultimately, capability.

Consistent Message

As George and Simons point out, clarity with respect to what is to be achieved through coercion is important in order to give policy makers a choice from among several response options, as well as providing clarity and consistency in what is being demanded to help persuade the opponent of the coercer's strength of purpose.[38] Without a consistent demand, an adversary is encouraged to counter the coercion, wait out or simply ignore the demand. Kosovo and Libya are examples of consistent US demands, while Panama and Bosnia provide cases of hesitant and changing demands. Coercion attempts with Panama and Bosnia could have been resolved sooner with steady, consistent demands backed by escalating, credible instruments of power.

---

[37] Byman and Waxman, 28.

[38] Alexander L. George and William E. Simons, *The Limits of Coercive Diplomacy (*Boulder: Westview Press, 1994), 280.

Credible

As Pape points out, "extremely high credibility that the coercer will impose damage is normally a minimum requirement."[39] How the coercer approaches the conflict as well as how the coercer has responded in the past affect the coercee's decision-making. In each case where the US has shown hesitance to use force, the credibility of the threat of force is reduced. Throughout the 1990s, the US was unable to coerce Iraq with limited airstrikes, which led Milosevic in Serbia to feel the threat of air strikes could be beaten.[40] Also, US officials limiting force options at the outset to minimize cost, and placing arbitrary timelines on the effort, negatively impact credibility of issued threats. Byman and Waxman note that will and credibility often matter more than the balance of forces, with casualty sensitivity, limited coalition cohesion and reluctance to commit high levels of military force reducing them.[41] The adversary must think all options are open to the coercer and believe the threat is real. In Bosnia and Kosovo, the deployment of US troops for peacekeeping may have helped add credibility to coercion if the Serbians had not known how, or if, ground troops would be used at the outset. In each case, assurances of no military intervention, statements reducing capability of the issued threat, public disagreement among senior government officials and between allies on the use of force all reduce the credibility of threatened force and negate capability.

---

[39] Robert A. Pape, *Bombing to Win: Air Power and Coercion in War* (Ithaca: Cornell University Press, 1996), 17.

[40] Dag Henricksen, "Inflexible Response: Diplomacy, Airpower and the Kosovo Crisis, 1998-1999," *The Journal of Strategic Studies* 31, no. 6 (December 2008): 839.

[41] Byman and Waxman, 18, 229.

Capable

There is little doubt in the capability of US forces when the will to use force exists. Publicly removing the threat of entire military components reduces the capability of the force, making US forces less effective in coercion attempts. Also, when the US joins coalitions, competing interests, capabilities, and willingness of coalition members to impose threatened punishments make the threats less capable through limitations imposed. Coercive instruments have shown to work better in concert rather than a single instrument. Keeping options open, along with devising a strategy the force can accomplish, will ensure the instruments available to the coercer are capable to execute the threats issued.

CHAPTER 5: CONCLUSION

To accomplish foreign policy goals without resorting to war, the United States (US) will need to employ coercion to shape the environment to favor US interests. Successfully coercing nations to comply with US demands will require developing a clear strategy, with realistic and consistent goals, along with credible means to issue threats of escalating force that are capable of imposing the stated objectives. A credible and capable military instrument of power is a key to successful coercion.

Coercion attempts to manipulate an adversary's behavior to comply with demands levied by the coercer. The coercer uses the elements of national power to deter or, if necessary compel acceptance. Compellence is obtained by increasing the perceived or real cost of behavior to exceed the benefits gained by the adversary. Therefore, the coercer must develop a strategy that makes the adversary perceive the cost will be too high, as the adversary's perception is essential to alter unwanted behavior.

To increase the perception of cost, threats must be credible and capable in order to achieve escalation dominance over the adversary. Credibility is achieved by keeping all options available publicly, not unnecessarily limiting options or levels and types of force employed. Though force limits will likely be applied, keeping these limits secret from the adversary are important to winning the perception battle. Capability is achieved by making forces appear flexible to accomplish required missions. Eliminating undue public restrictions will make it more difficult for the adversary to counter the coercive force. However, threats should not be issued or implied unless the coercer has the will to employ the threat.

Political leaders will have greater success in remaining credible when they agree on when and how to employ US forces before making interventions in foreign affairs. The case studies show that actions or statements that reduce the appearance of commitment also reduce the credibility of US demands. Once credibility is undermined, the adversary will believe the US forces employed also lack the capability required to impose the unwanted demand. This lack of credibility and capability encourages the adversary to counter the coercion or simply wait until the coercer tires of the struggle.

As the United States continues to develop an effective strategy to conduct foreign relations in the post-Soviet Union, post-Cold War world, military power will continue to remain critical to supporting foreign diplomacy. This power will be employed through coercion and to be successful several actions must be consistent. First, US political leadership must determine the national interests and the objective of the coercion. Second, US leadership must develop a coercive strategy to know how it intends to use the elements of national power to achieve the objectives. Then the US must state the demand or objectives clearly, so the adversary understands what is required and believes the US commitment. Third, leadership should only directly threaten elements they intend to use, however no options should be eliminated publicly. This keeps the adversary guessing while maintaining credibility in what is stated. Finally, pressure must increase until the adversary complies, conditions change or, if necessary, military force imposes the acceptable solution.

As shown, a consistent demand backed by credible and capable threats of US military power are essential to successful coercion as part of US foreign policy success.

Properly and consistently using this instrument, along with other elements of national

power, can better achieve the desired security strategy for the nation.

BIBLIOGRAPHY

Albright, Madeline, with Bob Woodward. *Madame Secretary.* New York: Miramax Books, 2003.

Bartlett, Henry C., G. Paul Holmann and Timothy E. Somes. "The Art and Strategy of Force Planning," In *Strategy and Force Planning,* 17-33. Newport: Naval War College Press, 2004.

Berry, Mary Frances and Josh Gottheimer. *Power in Words: The Stories Behind Barak Obama's Speeches, From the State House to the White House.* Boston: Beacon Books, 2010.

Bert, Wayne. *The Reluctant Superpower: United States Policy in Bosnia, 1991-1995.* New York: St. Martin's Press, 1997.

Betts, Richard K. "Are Civil-Military Relations Still a Problem?" In *American Civil-Military Relations: The Soldier and the State in a New Era,* 11-41. Baltimore: The Johns Hopkins University Press, 2009.

Branch, Taylor. *The Clinton Tapes: Wrestling History with the President.* New York: Simon and Schuster, 2009.

Byman, Daniel and Matthew Waxman. *The Dynamics of Coercion: American Foreign Policy and the Limits of Military Might.* New York: Cambridge University Press, 2002.

Chollet, Derek and Bennett Freeman. *The Secret History of Dayton: US Diplomacy and the Bosnian Peace Process 1995.* Washington DC: The National Security Archive, George Washington University, 2005. http://www.gwu.edu/~nsarchiv/NSAEBB/NSAEBB171/index.htm (accessed November 14, 2011).

Cimbala, Stephen J. *The Dead Volcano: The Background and Effects of Nuclear War Complacency.* Westport, CT: Preager Publishers, 2002.

Clark, Wesley K. *Waging Modern War: Bosnia, Kosovo, and the Future of Combat.* New York: Public Affairs, 2001.

Clausewitz, Carl Von. *On War.* Indexed edition. Translated by Michael Howard and Peter Paret. Princeton: Princeton University Press, 1976.

Cole, Ronald H. *Operation JUST CAUSE: The Planning and Execution of Joint Operations in Panama, February 1988 – January 1990.* Washington DC: Joint History Office, 1995.

Congressional Research Service, *Bosnia: Current Issues and US Policy, A Study Prepared for Members and Committees of Congress by the Congressional Research Service, June, 2011.* Washington DC: Government Printing Office, 2011.

Congressional Research Service. *Kosovo: Review and Analysis of Policy Objectives, 1998-Jun 1999: A Study Prepared for Members and Committees of Congress by the Congressional Research Service, July 1999.* Washington DC: Government Printing Office, 1999.

Congressional Research Service, *Libya: Unrest and U.S Policy: A Study Prepared for Members and Committees of Congress, by the Congressional Research Service, March 2011.* Washington DC: Government Printing Office, 2011.

Daadler, Ivo H. and Michael E. O'Hanlon. *Winning Ugly: NATO's War to Save Kosovo.* Washington DC: Brookings Institution Press, 2000.

Douhet, Giulio. *The Command of the Air.* Translated by Dino Ferrari. North Stratford: Ayer Company Publishers, Inc., 2002.

Democratic Leadership Council, "A New Covenant for American Security: address at Georgetown University," http://www.dlc.org/ndol_ci.cfm?kaid=128&subid=174&contentid=250537 (accessed January 15, 2012).

Department of Defense. *Report of the DoD Commission on Beirut International Airport Terrorist Attack, 23 Oct 1983*, by Admiral (Ret) Robert L. Long. Department of Defense. Washington D.C., November 1983.

Eccles, Henry E. *Military Power in a Free Society.* Newport: Naval War College Press, 1979.

Federal News Service, "Salon Luncheon with Former Secretary of State George Shultz, 29 October 2009," Carnegie Endowment for International Peace, http://carnegieendowment.org/files/1027carnegie-shultz (accessed 21 January 2012).

Flanagan, Edward M. Jr. *Battle for Panama: Inside Operation JUST CAUSE.* Washington DC: Brassey's (US), Inc., 1993.

Forage, Paul C. "Bombs for Peace: A Comparative Study of the Use of Air Power in the Balkans," *Armed Forces and Society* 28, No. 2 (Winter 2002): 211-32.

George, Alexander L., and Richard Smoke. *Deterrence in American Foreign Policy: Theory and Practice.* New York: Columbia University Press, 1974.

George, Alexander L., and William E. Simons. *The Limits of Coercive Diplomacy.* Boulder: Westview Press, 1994.

George Bush Presidential Library, "Inaugural Address, January 20, 1989," http://bushlibrary.tamu.edu/research/public_papers.php?id=1356&year=1989&month=all (accessed January 21, 2012).

George Bush Presidential Library, "White House address, December 20, 1989," http://bushlibrary.tamu.edu/research/public_papers.php?id=1356&year=1989&month=all (accessed January 21, 2012).

George Bush Presidential Library, "State of the Union address, January 20, 1991," http://bushlibrary.tamu.edu/research/public_papers.php?id=1356&year=1989&month=all (accessed January 21, 2012).

Gilboa, Eytan. "The Panama Invasion Revisited: Lessons for the Use of Force in the Post Cold War Era," *Political Science Quarterly* 110, no. 4 (Winter 1995): 539-62.

Gray, Colin S. *Hard Power and Soft Power: The Utility of Military Force as an Instrument of Policy in the 21st Century.* Carlisle: Strategic Studies Institute, April 2011.

Greenhill, Kelly M., *Weapons of Mass Migration: Forced Displacement, Coercion and Foreign Policy,* Ithaca: Cornell University Press, 2010.

Haass, Richard N. *Intervention: The Use of American Military Force in the Post-Cold War World,* revised edition. Washington DC: Brookings Institution Press, 1999.

Hamilton, Nigel. *Bill Clinton: Mastering the Presidency.* New York: Perseus Books Group, 2007.

Hammes, Thomas X. *The Sling and the Stone: On War in the 21st Century.* St Paul: Zenith Press, 2004.

Handel, Michael I. *Masters of War: Classic Strategic Thought, Third Edition.* Portland: Frank Cass Publishers, 2001.

Henricksen, Dag. "Inflexible Response: Diplomacy, Airpower and the Kosovo Crisis, 1998-1999," *The Journal of Strategic Studies* 31, no. 6 (December 2008): 836.

Herspring, Dale R. *The Pentagon and the Presidency: Civil Military Relations from FDR to George W. Bush.* Lawrence: University Press of Kansas, 2005.

Ignatieff, Michael. *Virtual War: Kosovo and Beyond.* New York: Metropolitan Books, 2000.

Institute for Defense Studies and Analysis. "US Role in Libya: Declining Hegemony?" Institute for Defense Studies and Analysis. http://www.idsa.in/idsacomments/USRoleinLibyaDecliningHegemony_bpothuraju_100511. (accessed 19 August 2011).

Johnson, David E., Karl P. Mueller and William H. Taft, V. *Conventional Coercion Across the Spectrum of Operations: The Utility of US Military Forces in the Emerging Security Environment.* Santa Monica: Rand, 2002.

Johnson, David E. *"Modern US Civil-Military Relations: Wielding the Terrible Swift Sword.* McNair Paper 57 (July 1997).

Judah, Tim. *Kosovo: War and Revenge.* New Haven: Yale University Press, 2000.

Kalyvas, Stathis N. and Nicholas Sambanis, "Bosnia's Civil War: Origins and Violence," In *Understanding Civil War,* vol 2, 191-229. Washington DC: Worldbank, 2005.

Kissinger, Henry. *Diplomacy.* New York: Simon and Schuster, 1994.

Library of Congress. "War Powers Resolution," Law Library of Congress, http://loc.gov/law/help/war-powers.pht (accessed March 21, 2012).

Lippman, Thomas W. *Madeline Albright and the New American Diplomacy* Boulder: Westview Press, 2002.

Mayers, David. *Wars and Peace: The Future Americans Envisioned.* New York: St. Martin's Press, 1998.

Means, Howard. *Colin Powell: Soldier/Statesman, Statesman/Soldier.* New York: Donald I. Fine, Inc., 1992.

Meernik, James D., *The Political Use of Military Force in US Foreign Policy,* Burlington: Ashgate Publishing Company, 2004.

Nielsen, Suzanne C., and Don M. Snider. *American Civil-Military Relations: The Soldier and the State in a New Era.* Baltimore: The Johns Hopkins University Press, 2009.

Owen, Robert C. "An American View of Peace Support Operations: A Perspective on Air Power," In *From Maneuver Warfare to Kosovo?* 115-136. Norway: The Royal Norwegian Air Force Academy, 2006.

Pape, Robert A., *Bombing to Win: Air Power and Coercion in War,* Ithaca: Cornell University Press, 1996.

Quayle, Dan., *Standing Firm: A Vice Presidential Memoir*, New York: Harper-Collins Publishers, 1994.

Record, Jeffrey. *Making War, Thinking History.* Annapolis: Naval Institute Press, 2002.

Rogel, Carole. *The Breakup of Yugoslavia and the War in Bosnia.* Westport: Greenwood Press, 1998.

Roth, David. *Sacred Honor: A Biography of Colin Powell.* Grand Rapids: Zondervan Publishing House, 1993.

Rubintstein, Alvin Z., Albina Shayevich and Boris Zlotnikov, *The Clinton Foreign Policy Reader: Presidential Speeches with Commentary.* New York: M.E. Sharp, 2000.

Sale, Richard. *Clinton's Secret Wars The Evolution of a Commander in Chief.* New York: St Martin's Press, 2009.

Sharp, Ulysses S. Grant. *Strategy for Defeat: Vietnam in Retrospect.* Novato: Presidio Press, 1986.

Shelling, Thomas C., *Arms and Influence.* New Haven: Yale University Press, 1966.

Short, Michael C. "An Airman's Lessons from Kosovo," In *From Maneuver Warfare to Kosovo?* 257-288. Norway: The Royal Norwegian Air Force Academy, 2006.

Shultz, George P. "US Foreign Policy: Realism and Progress." *Vital Speeches of the Day* 49, no. 4 (December 1, 1982): 98-102.

Sun Tzu. *The Art of War.* Translated and with an introduction by Samuel B. Griffith. New York: Oxford University Press, 1971.

Strickland, Paul C. "Decisive or Coercive?" *Aerospace Power Journal.* (Fall 2000). http://www.airpower.maxwell.af.mil/airchronicles/apj/apj00/strickland.htm (accessed 19 August 2011).

Taw, Jennifer M. *Operation JUST CAUSE: Lessons for Operations Other Than War.* Santa Monica: Rand, 1996.

The White House. "The President on Libya: Our Goal is Focused, Our Cause Just, and Our Coalition is Strong." The White House Blog. http://www.whitehouse.gov/blog/2011/03/18/president-libya-our-goal-focused-our-cause-just-our-coalition-strong.htm (accessed 19 August 2011).

The White House. "The President on Libya: Today We are Part of a Broad Coalition, We are Answering the Calls of a Threatened People, and Acting in the Interests of the United States and the World." The White House Blog.

http://www.whitehouse.gov/blog/2011/03/20/remarks-president-libya.htm
(accessed 19 August 2011).

The White House. "The President on Libya: We Have Already Saved Lives." The White
House Blog. http://www.whitehouse.gov/blog/2011/03/18/president-libya-we-
have-already-saved-lives.htm (accessed 19 August 2011).

The White House. "Weekly address: The Mission in Libya is Succeeding." The White
House Blog. http://www.whitehouse.gov/blog/2011/03/26/president-obama-
mission-in-libya-is-succeeding.htm (accessed 19 August 2011).

The White House. "Remarks by the President in Address to the Nation on Libya." The
White House Blog. http://www.whitehouse.gov/blog/2011/03/28/remarks-
president-address-nation-libya-.htm (accessed 19 August 2011).

Tse-Tung, Mao. *On Guerilla Warfare.* Translated by Samuel B. Griffith, II. Urbana, IL:
University of Illinois Press, 1961.

United Nations Security Council, "Resolution 713, Cease Fire in Bosnia and Wepons
Embargo in Yugoslavia," UNSC. http://www.un.org/documents/res.htm,
(accessed January 15, 2012).

United Nations Security Council, "Resolution 743, Authorized a UN Protection Force,"
UNSC. http://www.un.org/documents/res.htm, (accessed January 15, 2012).

United Nations Security Council, "Resolution 752, Called for Yugoslavia and Croatia to
Stay out of Bosnia," UNSC. http://www.un.org/documents/res.htm, (accessed
January 15, 2012).

United Nations Security Council, "Resolution 816, No-fly Zone in Bosnia," "Resolution
904, Implemented Muslim Safe Zones," UNSC.
http://www.un.org/documents/res.htm, (accessed January 15, 2012).

United Nations Security Council, "Resolution 941, Demanded Ethnic Cleansing Cease,"
UNSC. http://www.un.org/documents/res.htm, (accessed January 15, 2012).

United Nations Security Council, "Resolution 1199, Kosovo Cease Fire," "Resolution
1203, Observers in Kosovo," UNSC. http://www.un.org/documents/res.htm,
(accessed January 15, 2012).

United Nations Security Council, "Resolution 1170, Sanctions on Libya," UNSC,
http://www.un.org/documents/res.htm, (accessed January 15, 2012).

United Nations Security Council, "Resolution 1973, Authorized Force to Enforce a No-
fly Zone," UNSC http://www.un.org/documents/res.htm, (accessed January 15,
2012).

United Nations Security Council, "Resolution 2016, Recognized Transitional Government," UNSC, http://www.un.org/documents/res.htm, (accessed January 15, 2012).

US Joint Chiefs of Staff, *Joint Operation Planning.* Joint Publication 5-0. Washington DC: Joint Chiefs of Staff, August 11, 2011.

US President. *A National Security Strategy for a New Century.* Washington DC: Government Printing Office, 1998.

US President. *National Security Strategy.* Washington D.C.: Government Printing Office, May 2010.

Warshaw, Shirley Anne. *Presidential Profiles: The Clinton Years.* New York: Facts on File, Inc., 2004.

Weinberger, Caspar W. *Fighting for Peace: Seven Critical Years in the Pentagon.* New York: Warner Books, 1990.

William J. Clinton Presidential Library, "PDD/NSC-25: US Policy on Reforming Multilateral Peace Operations," Clinton Presidential Library. http://www.clintonlibrary.gov/_previous/Documents/2010%20FOIA/Presidential%20Directives/PDD-25.pdf (accessed January 15, 2012).

www.ingramcontent.com/pod-product-compliance
Lightning Source LLC
Chambersburg PA
CBHW080317290526
45790CB00005B/2081